Skinny Girls

Hot Sexy Skinny Lingerie Girls Models Pictures

By **EROTICA PHOTO ART LOVER**

Copyright © Skinny Girls

All rights reserved. No part of this document may be Reproduced or transmitted in any form or by any means, electronic, mechanical, photocopying, Recording, or otherwise, without prior written permission of erotica photo art lover.

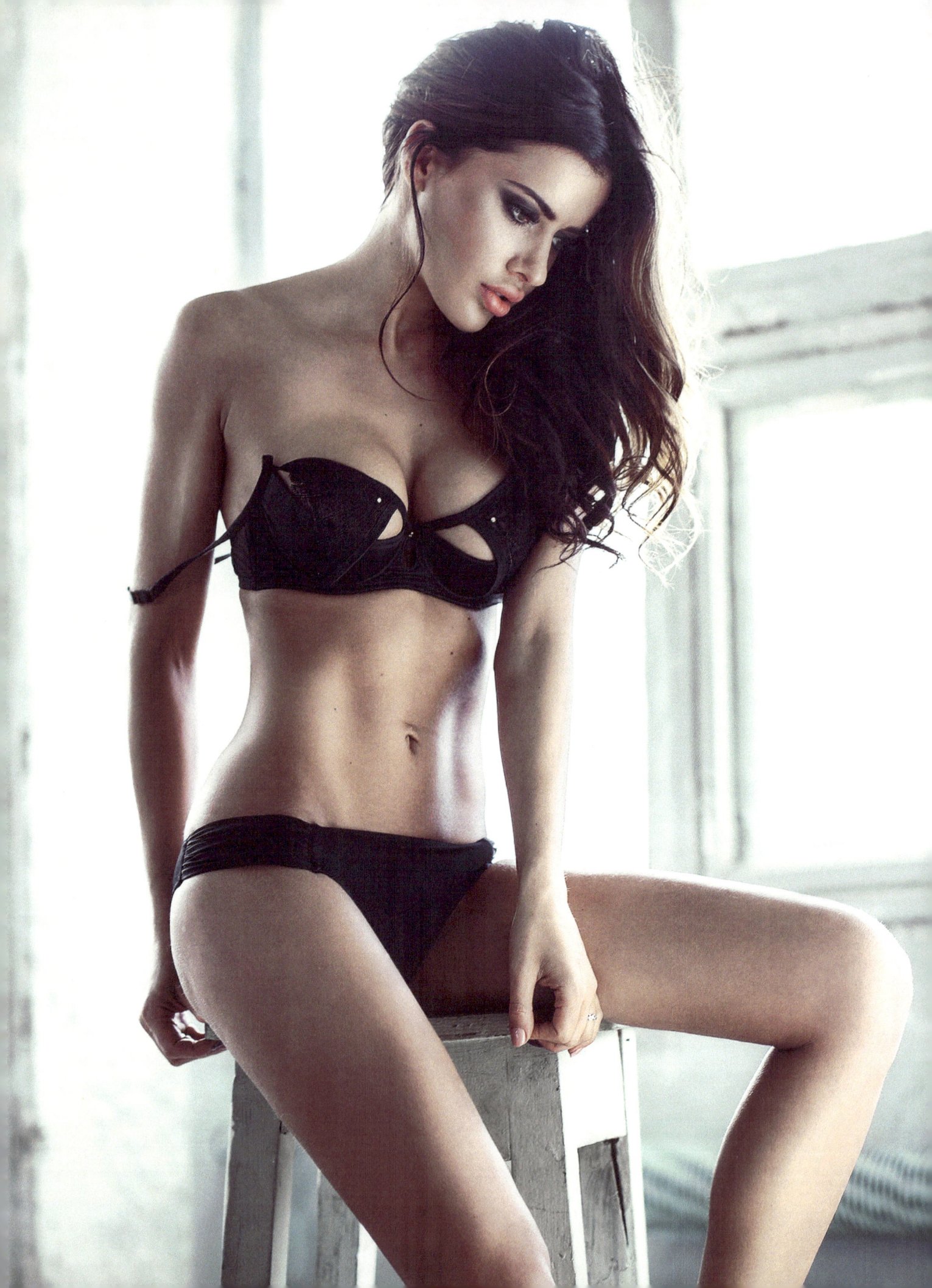

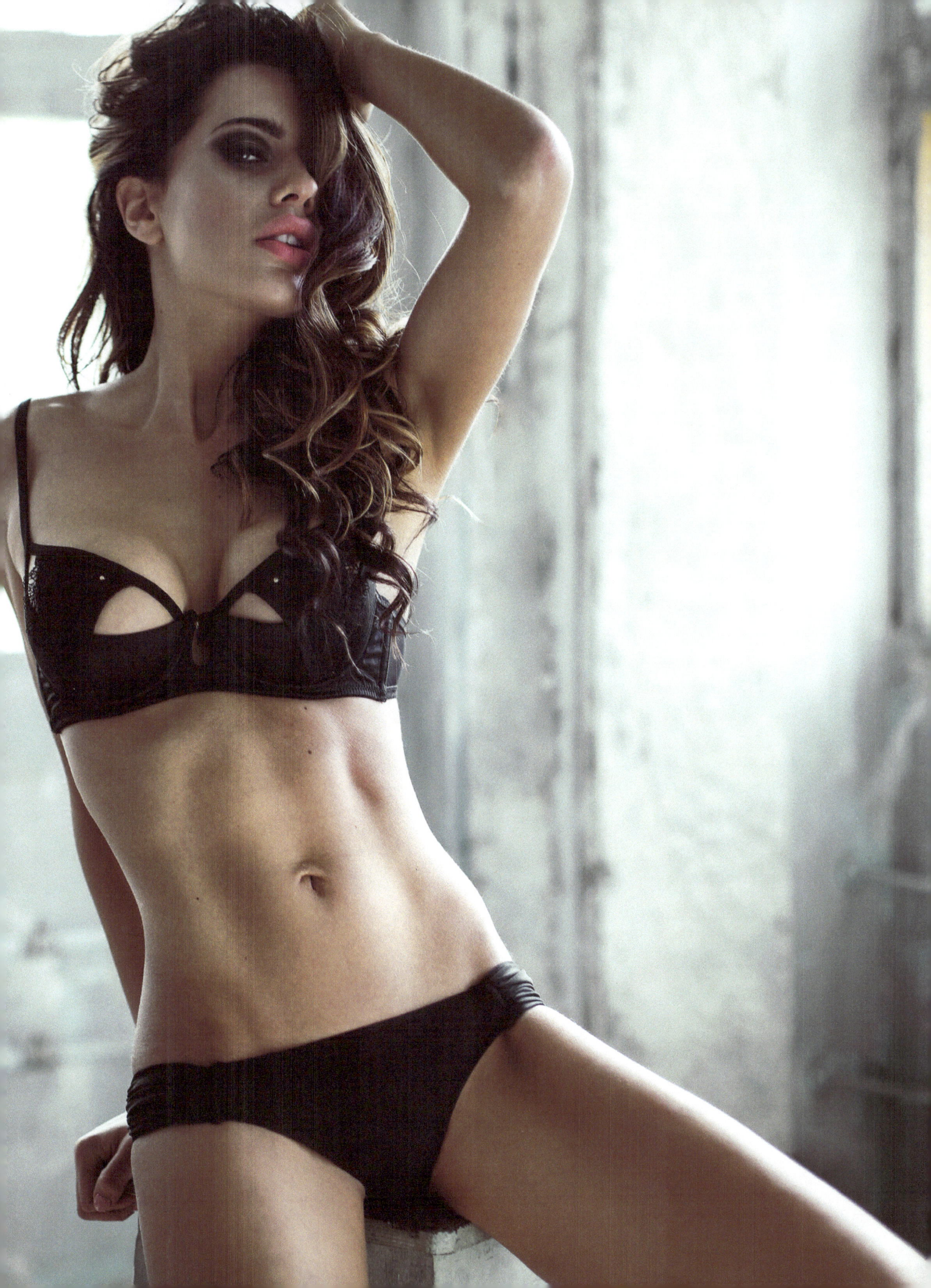

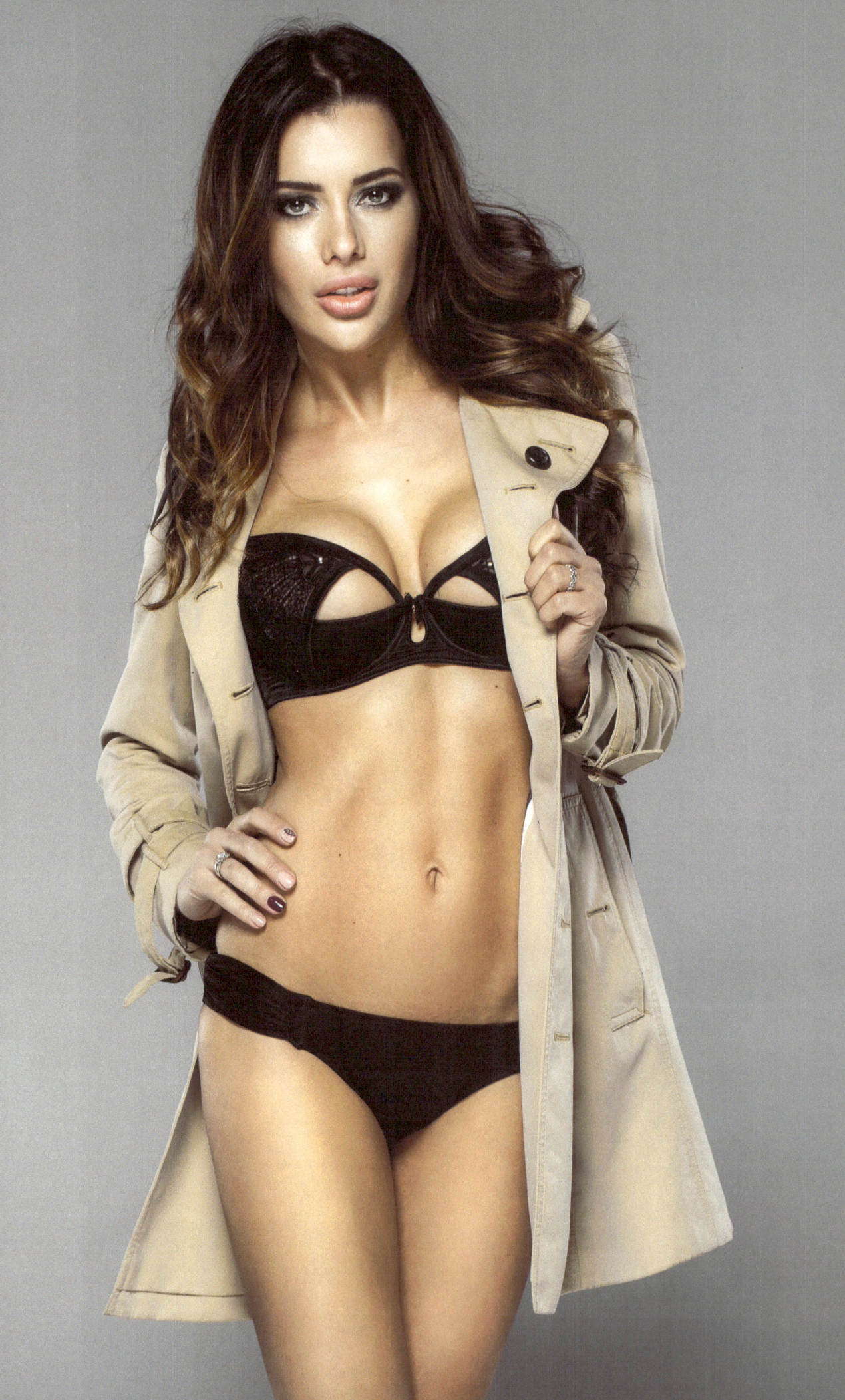

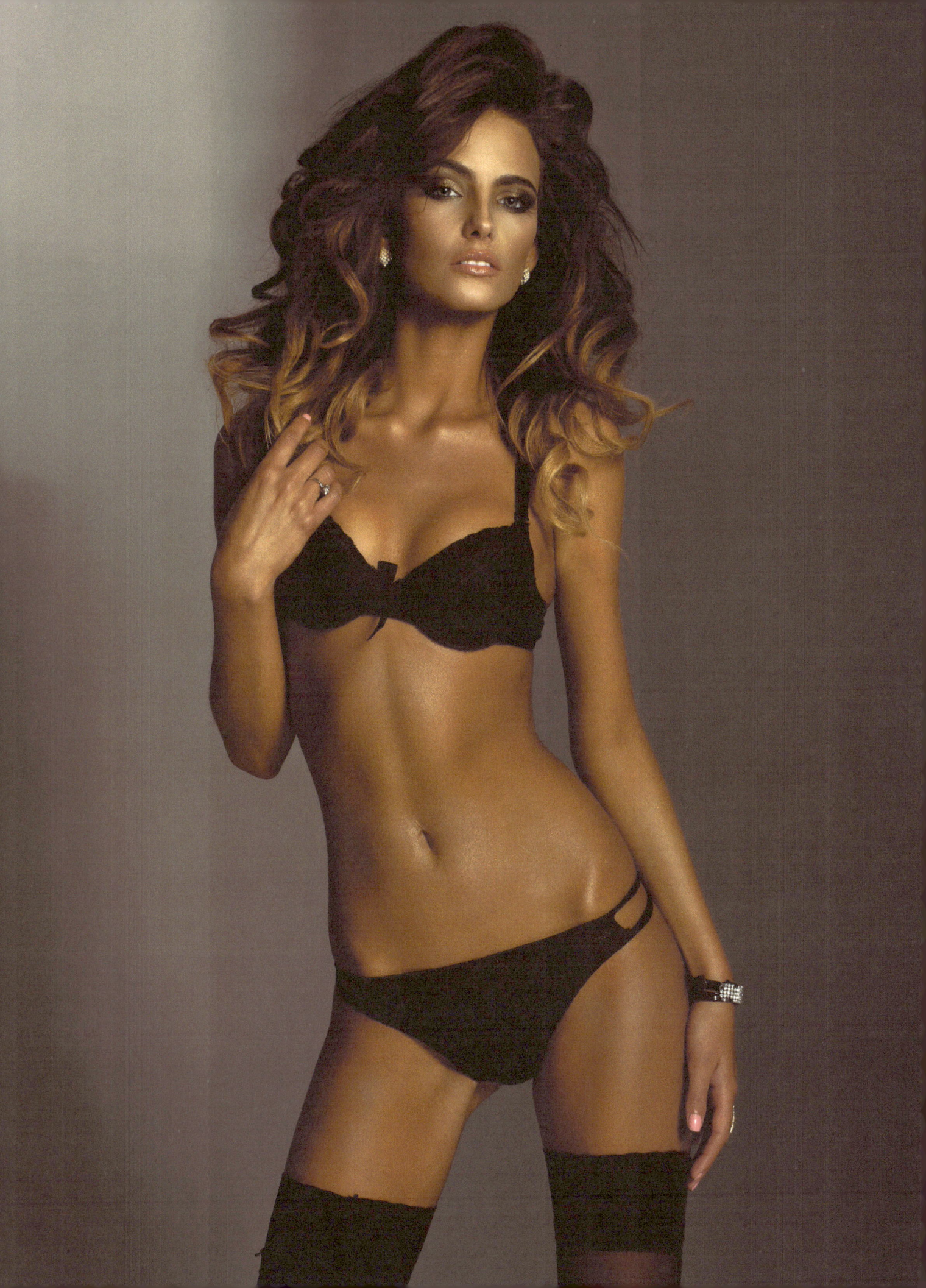

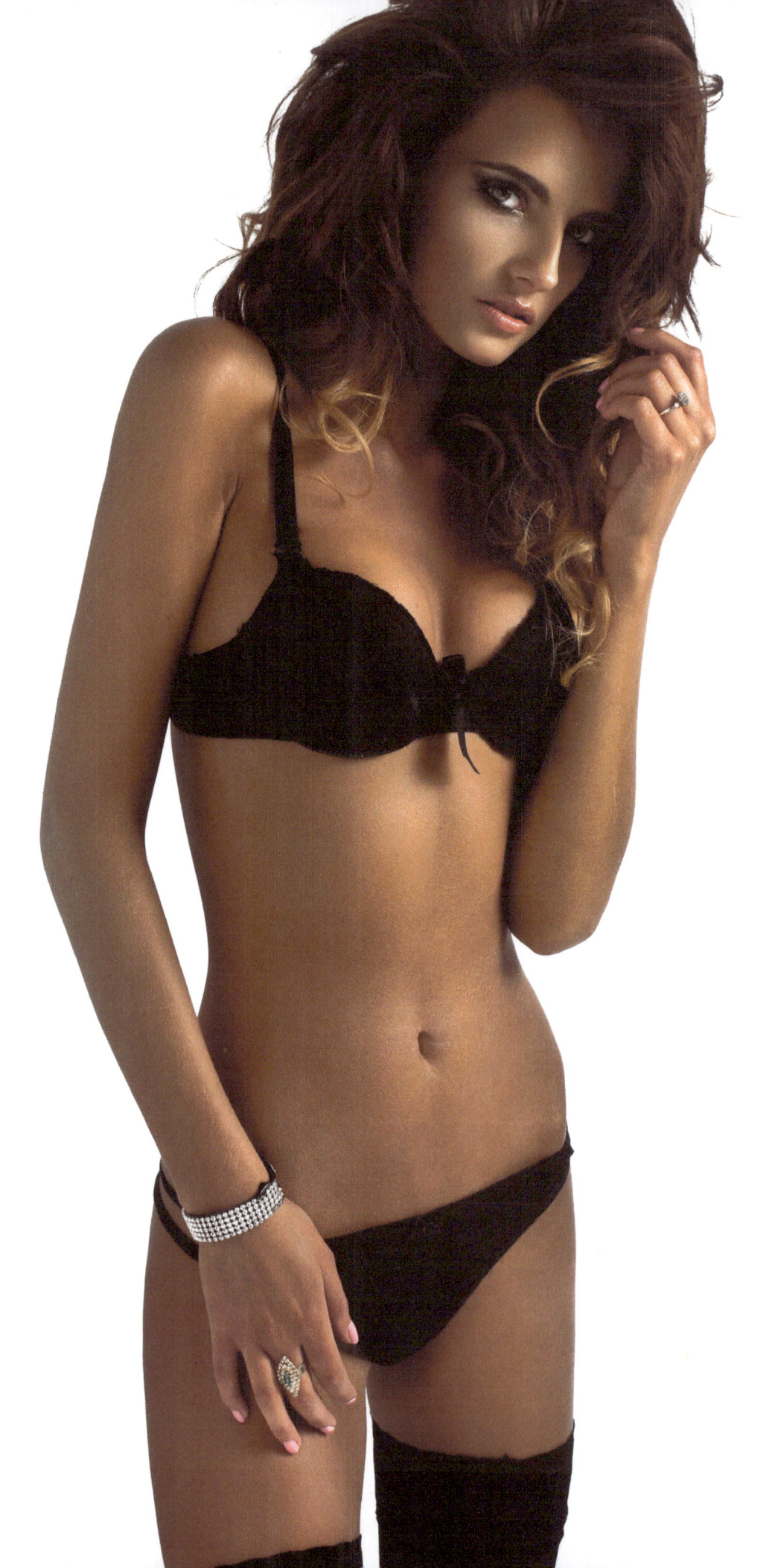

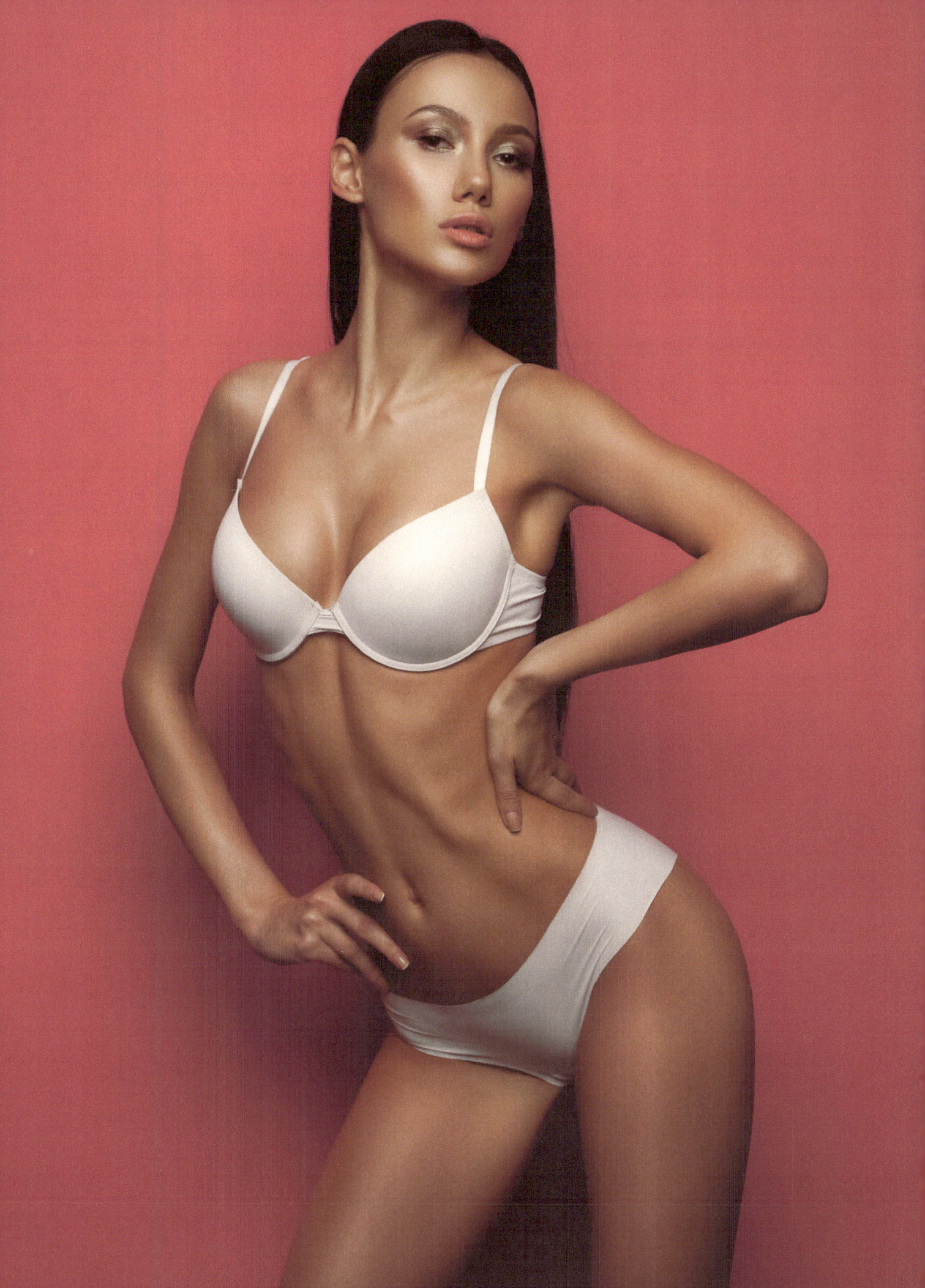

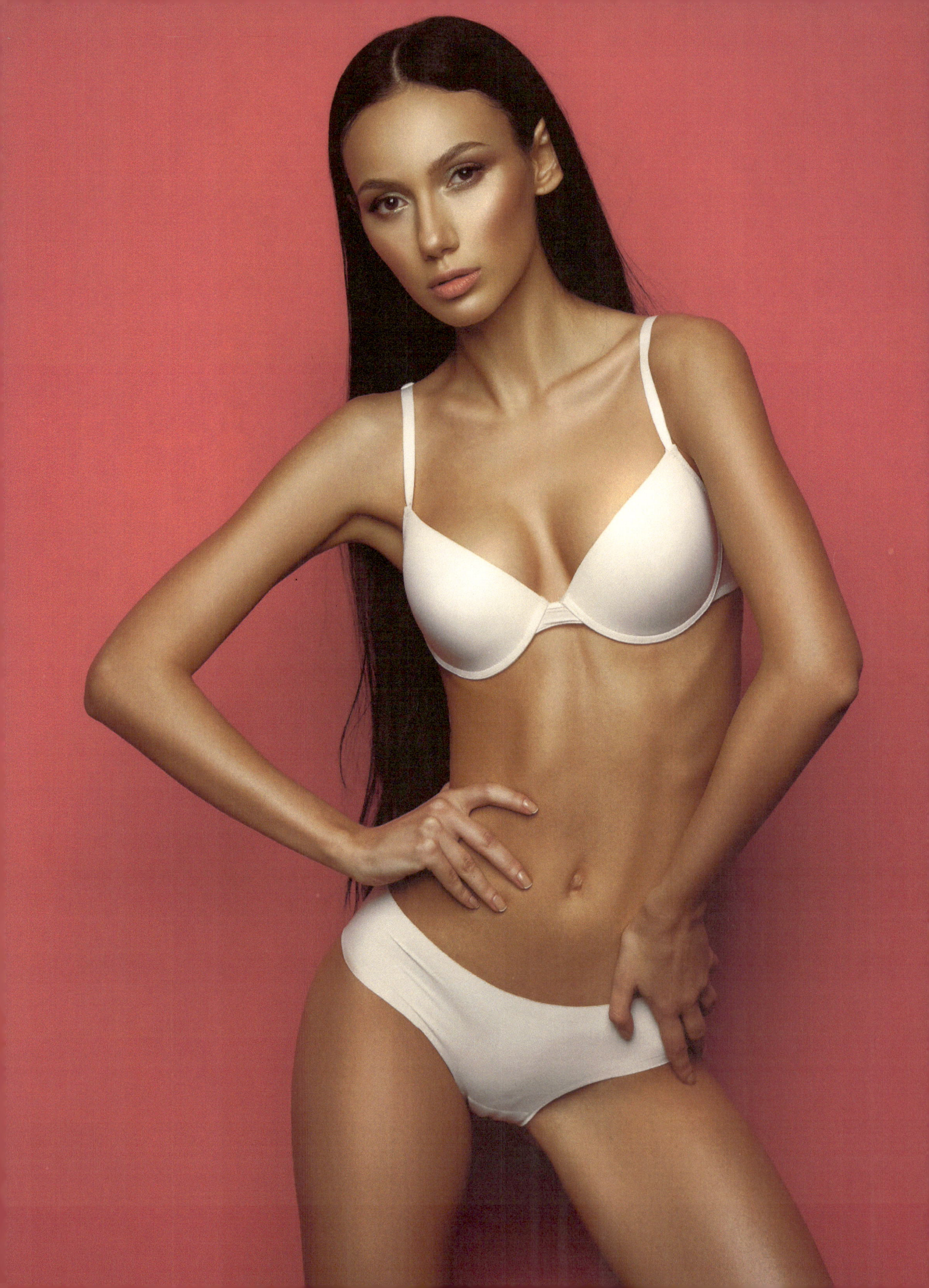

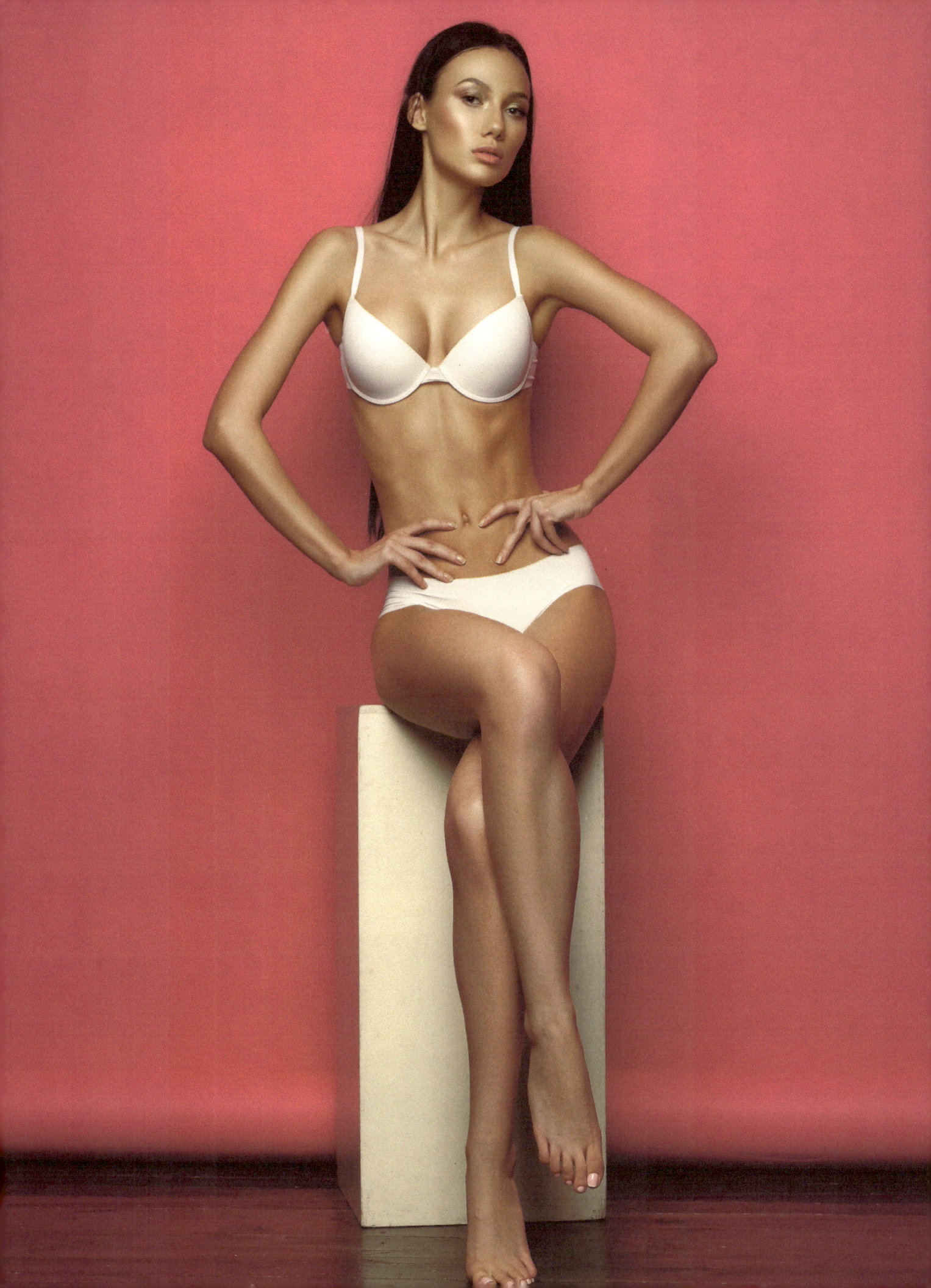

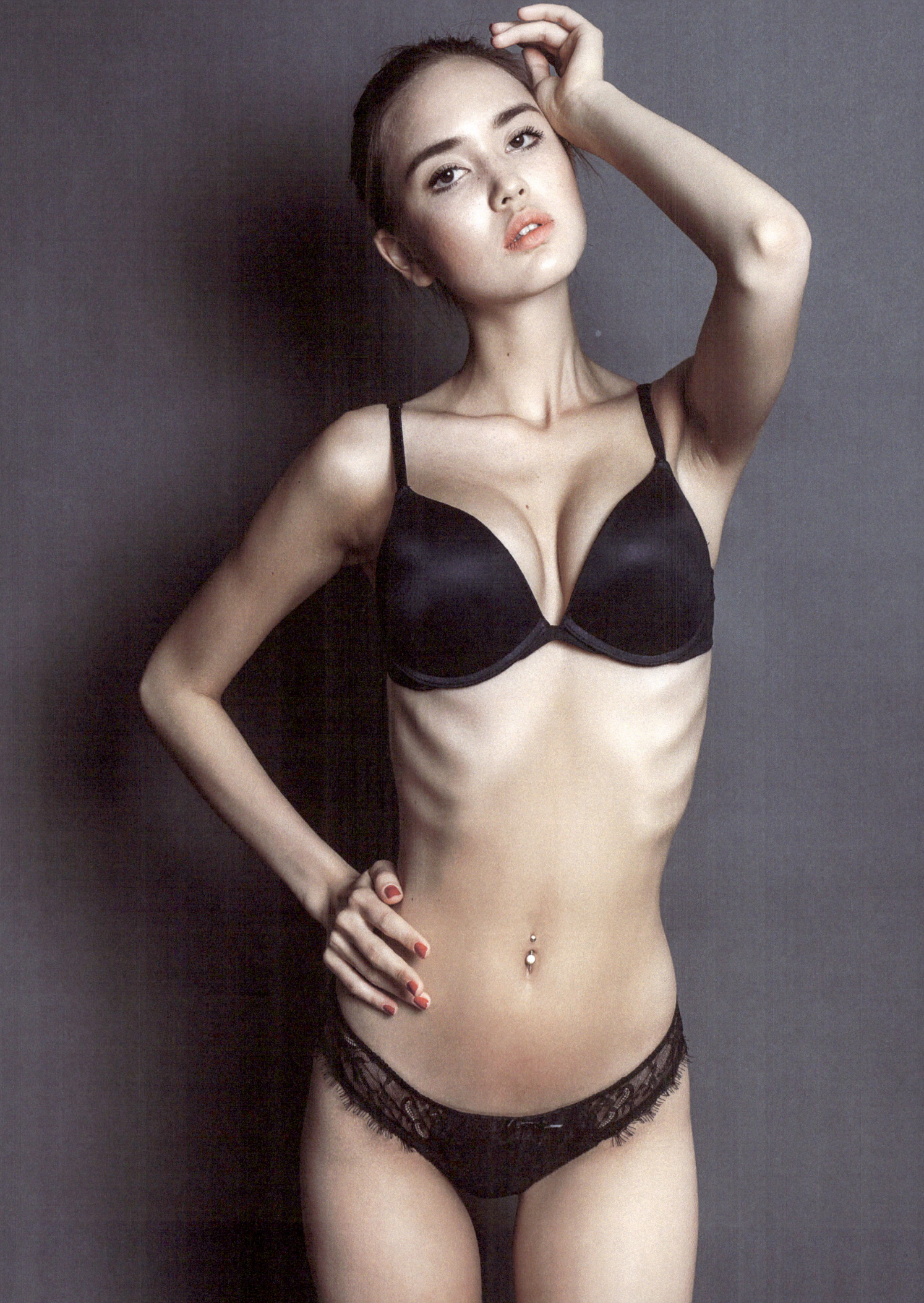

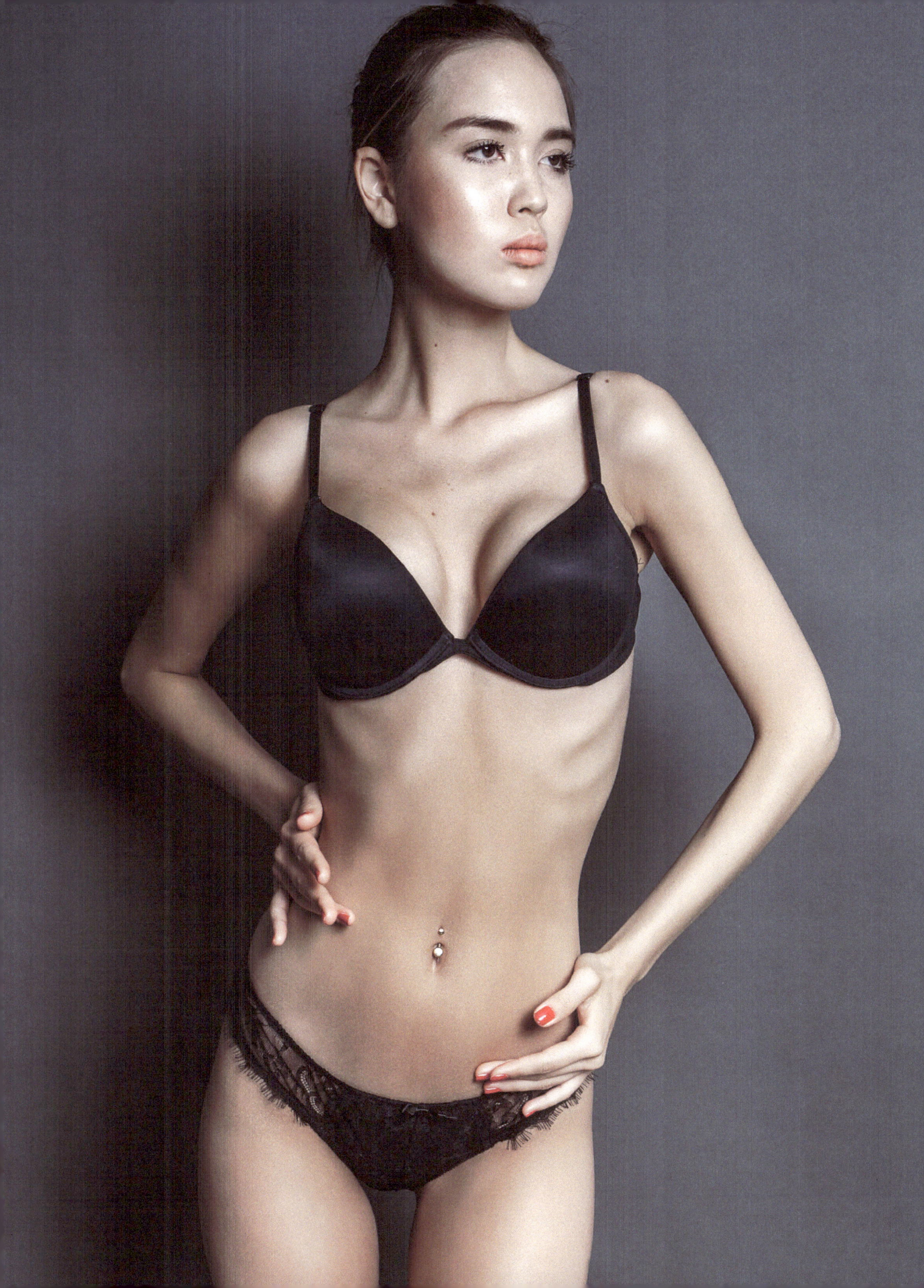

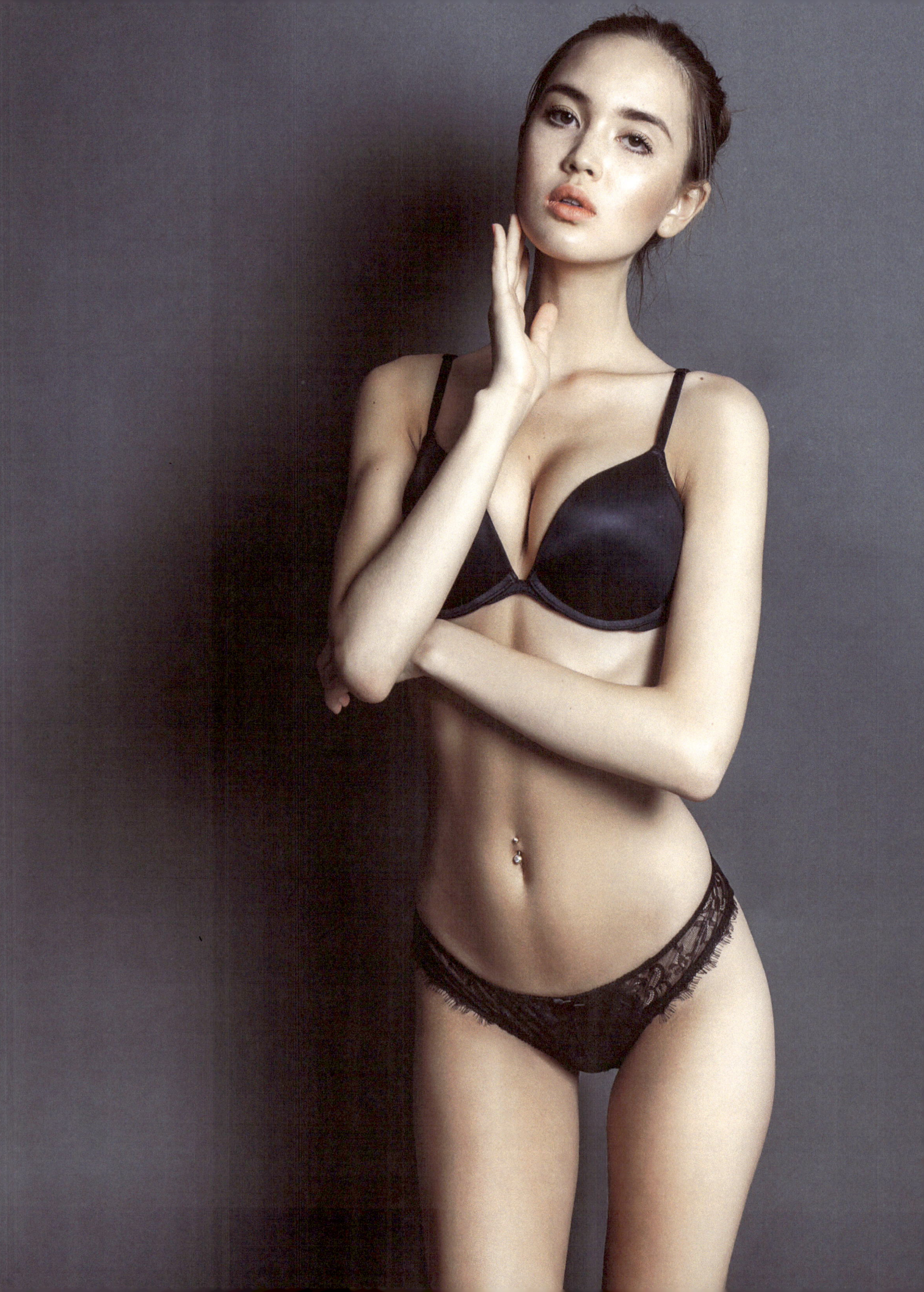

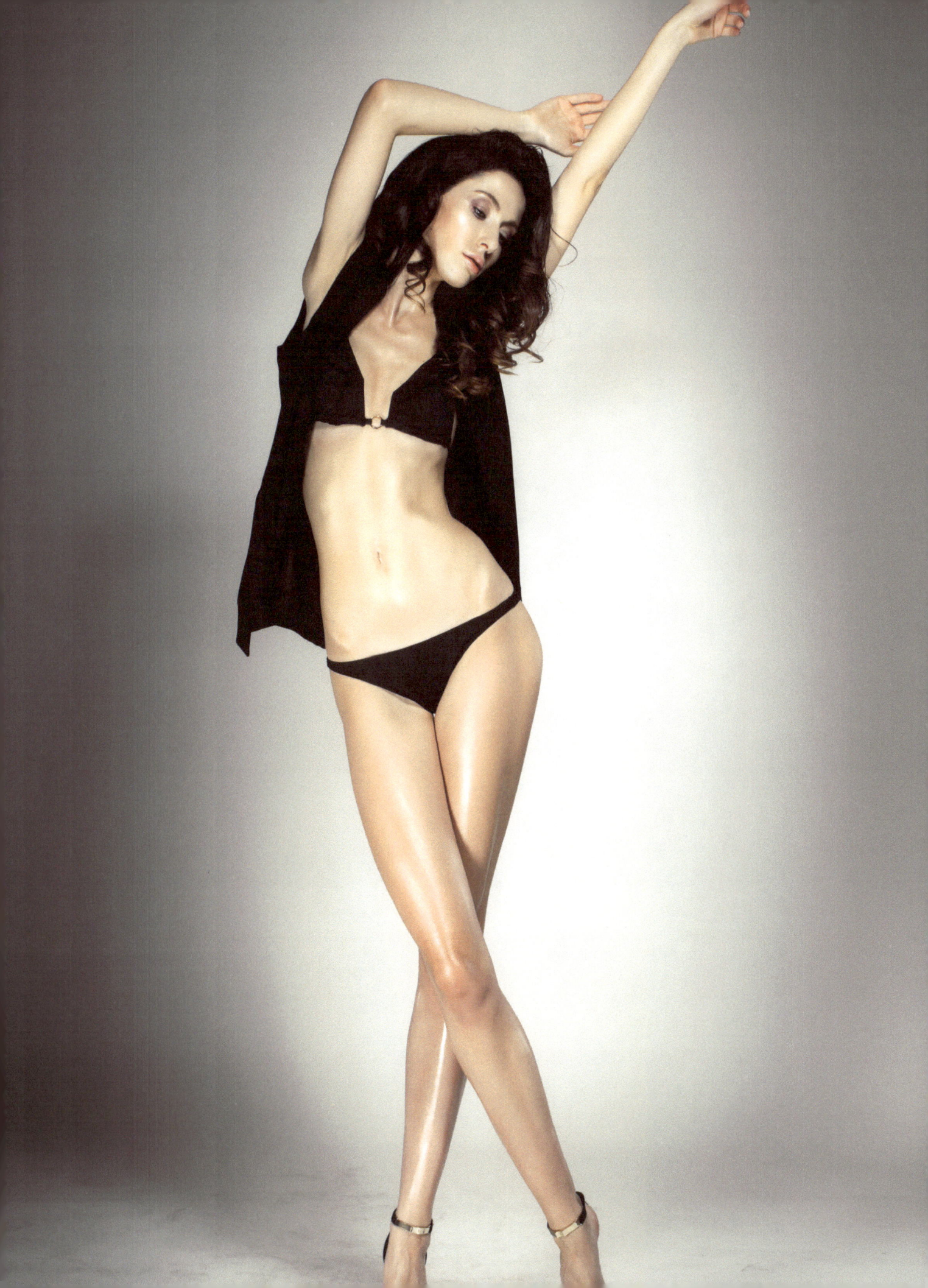

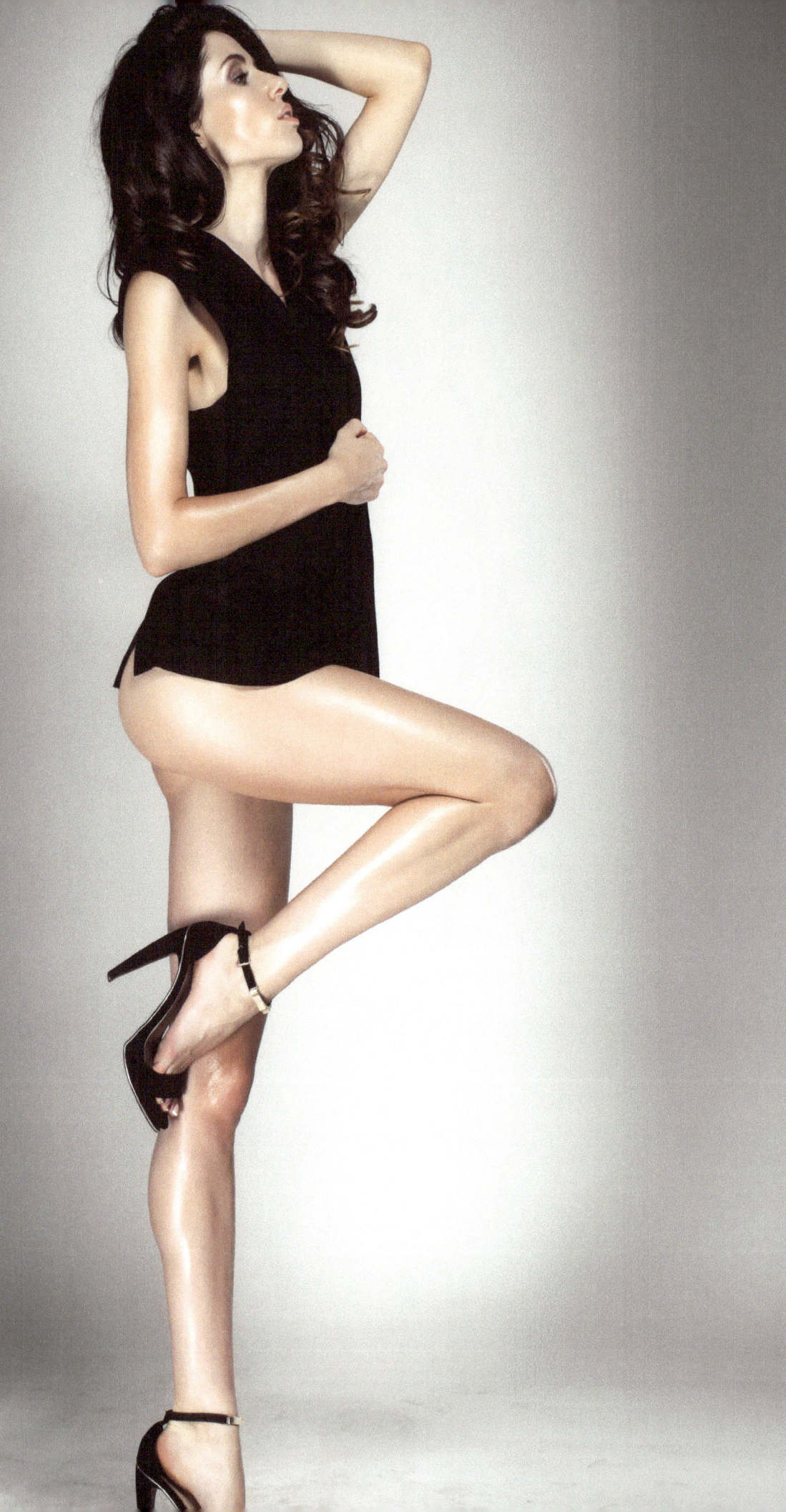

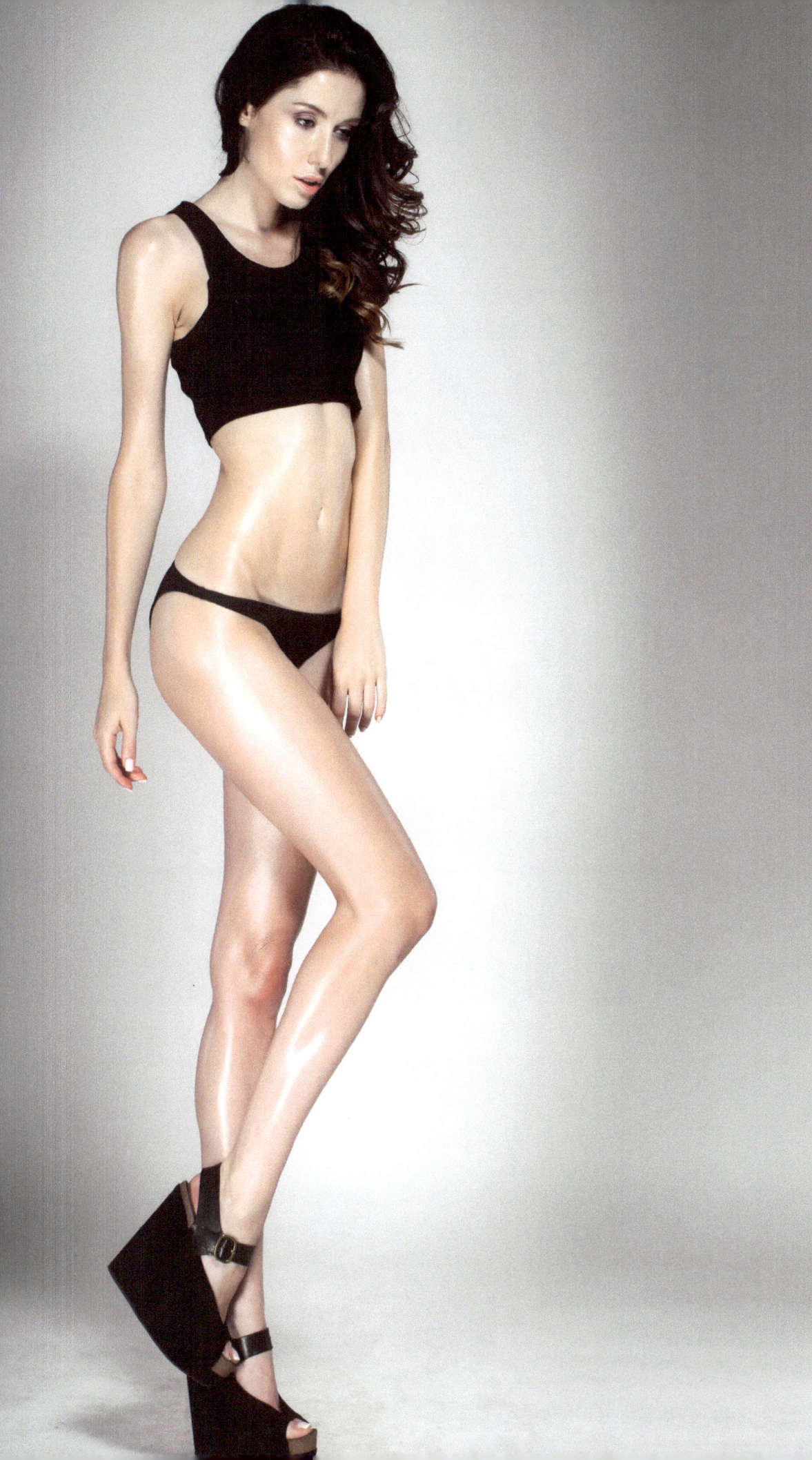

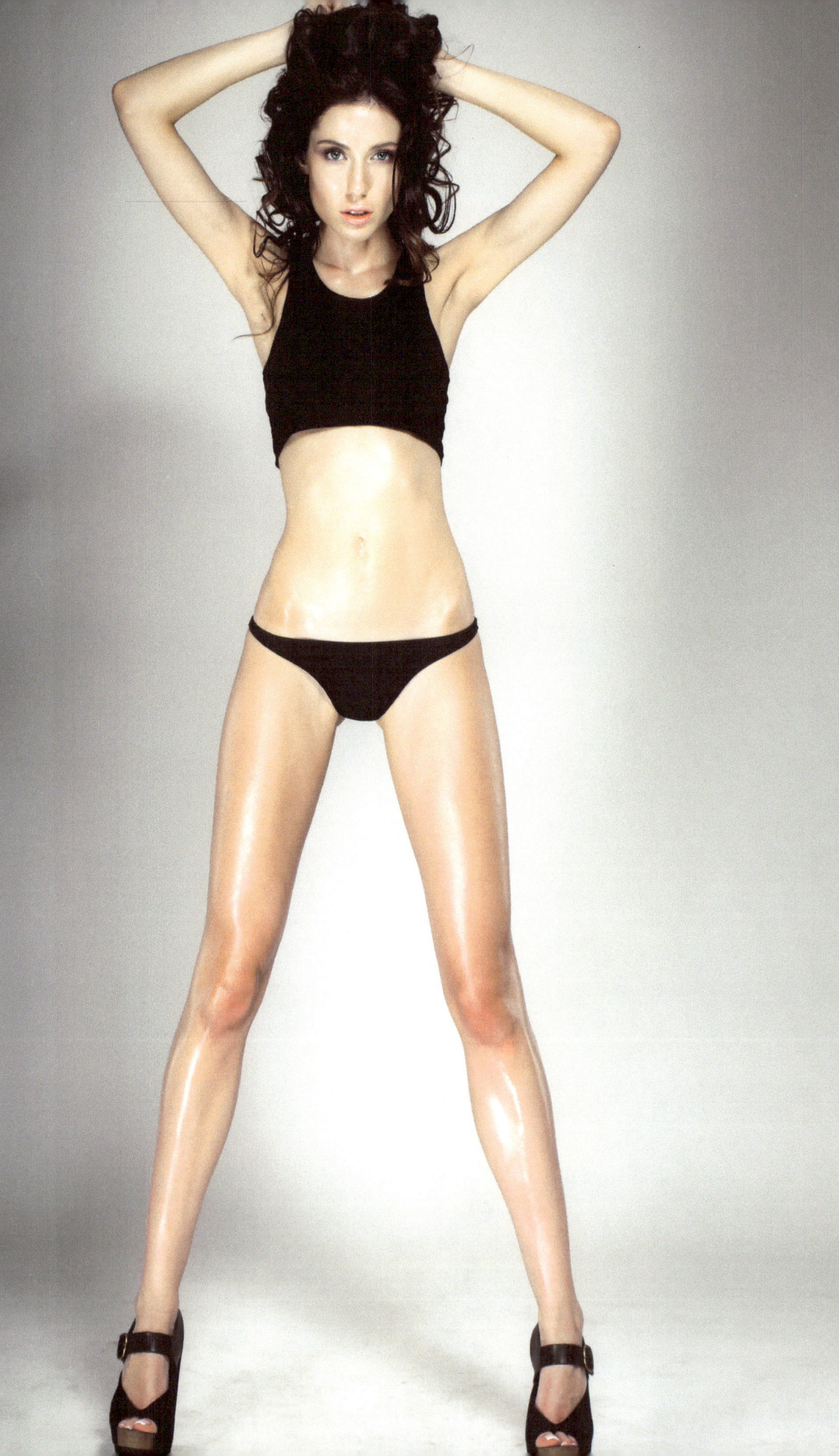

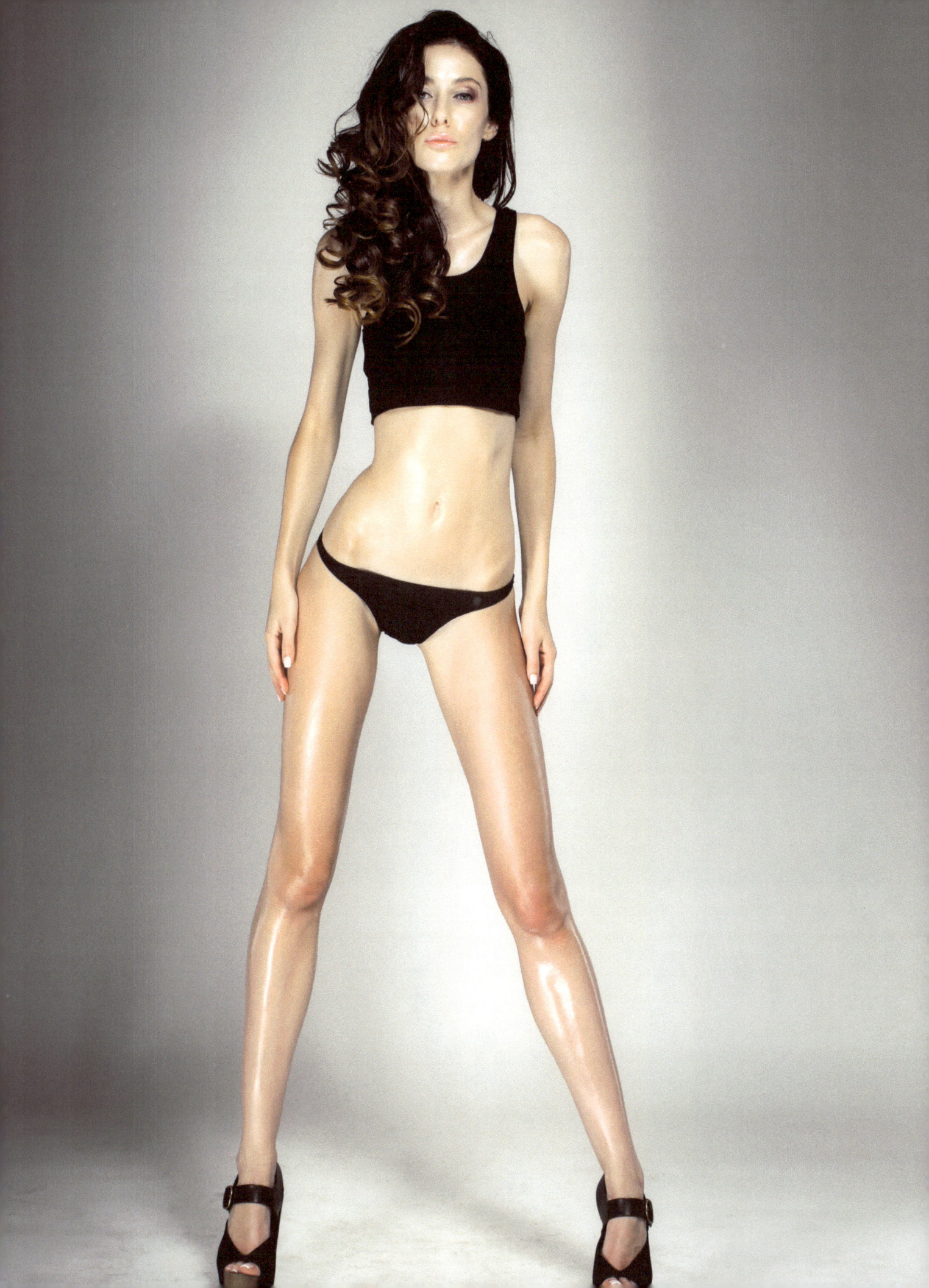

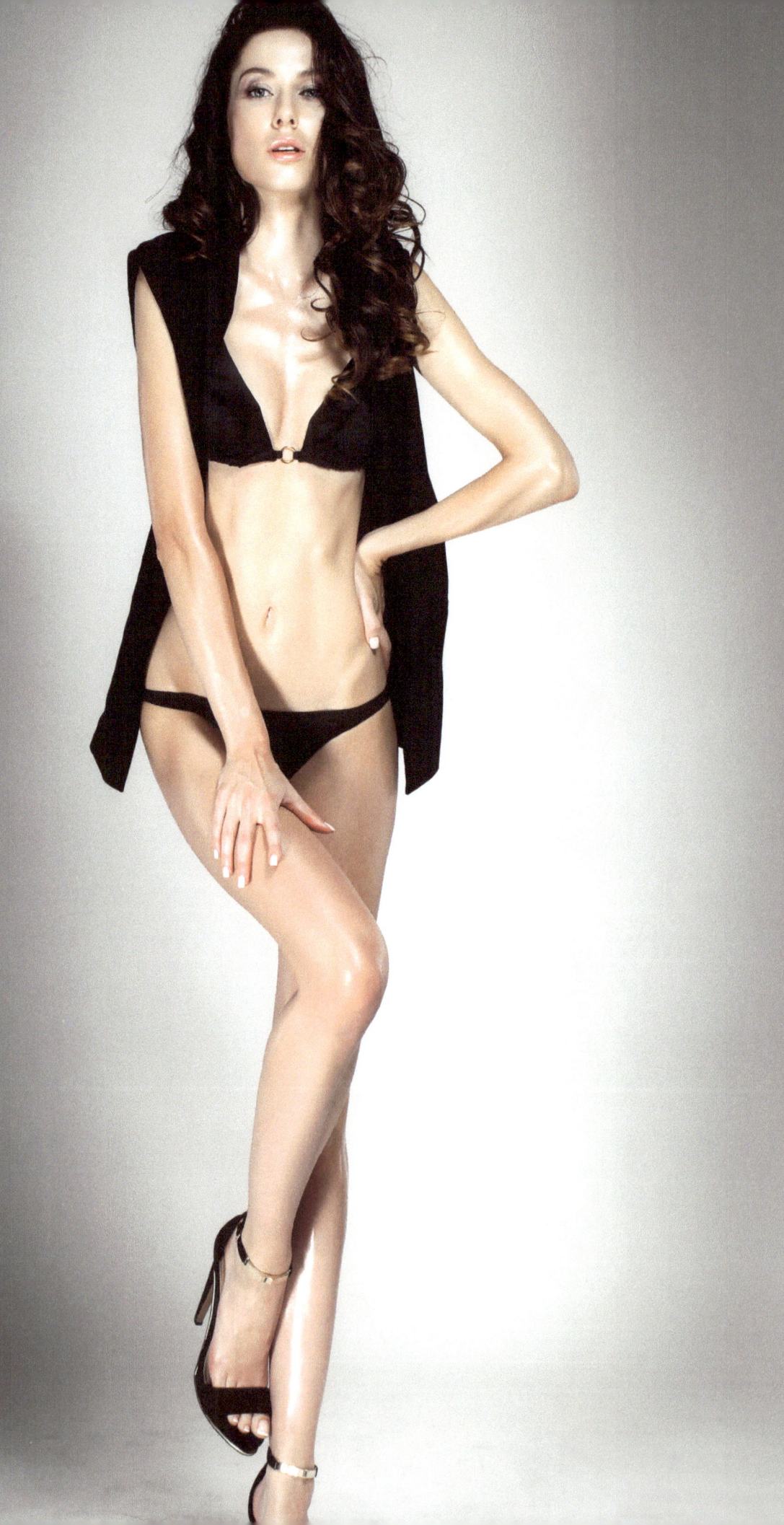

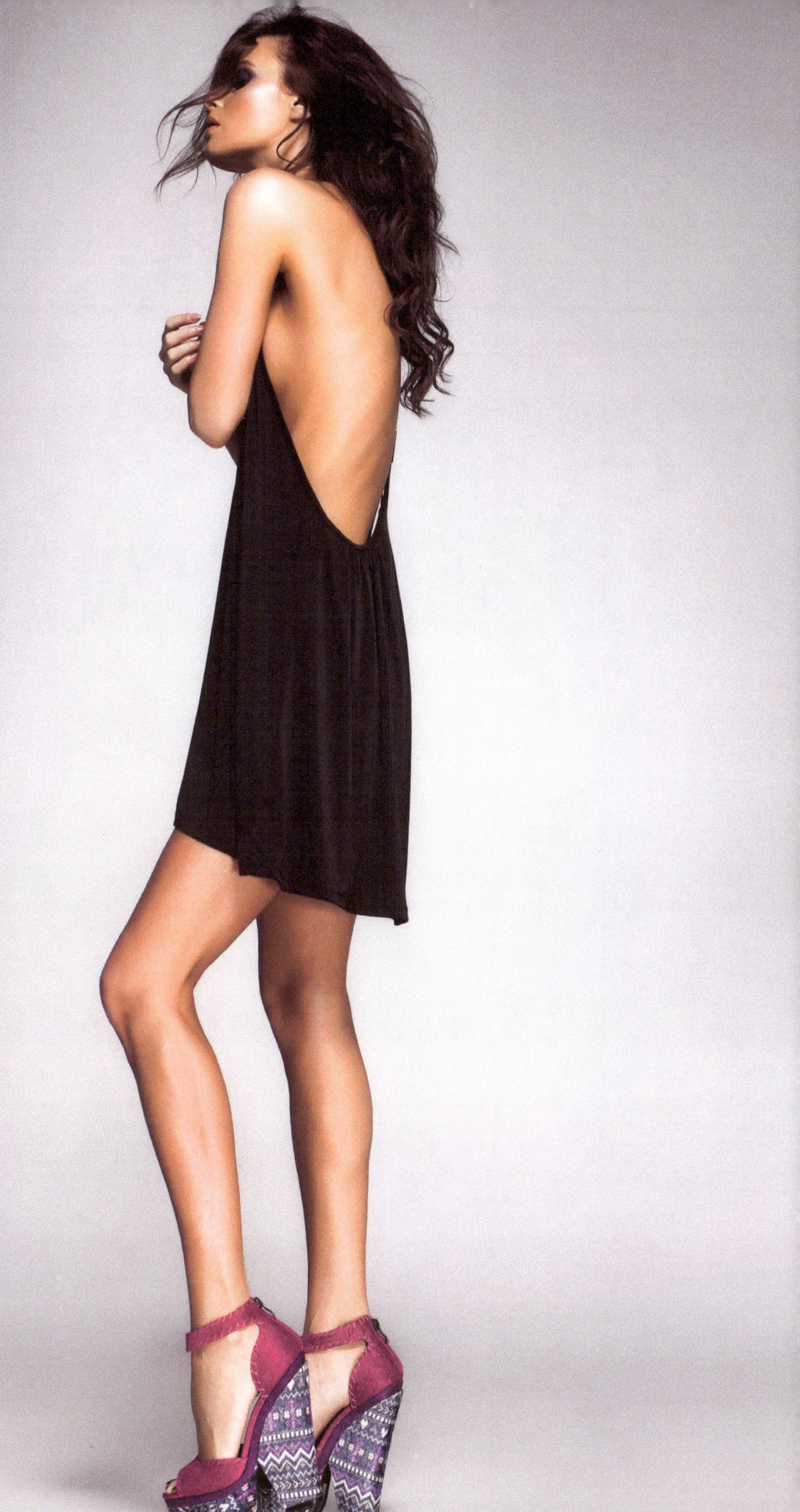

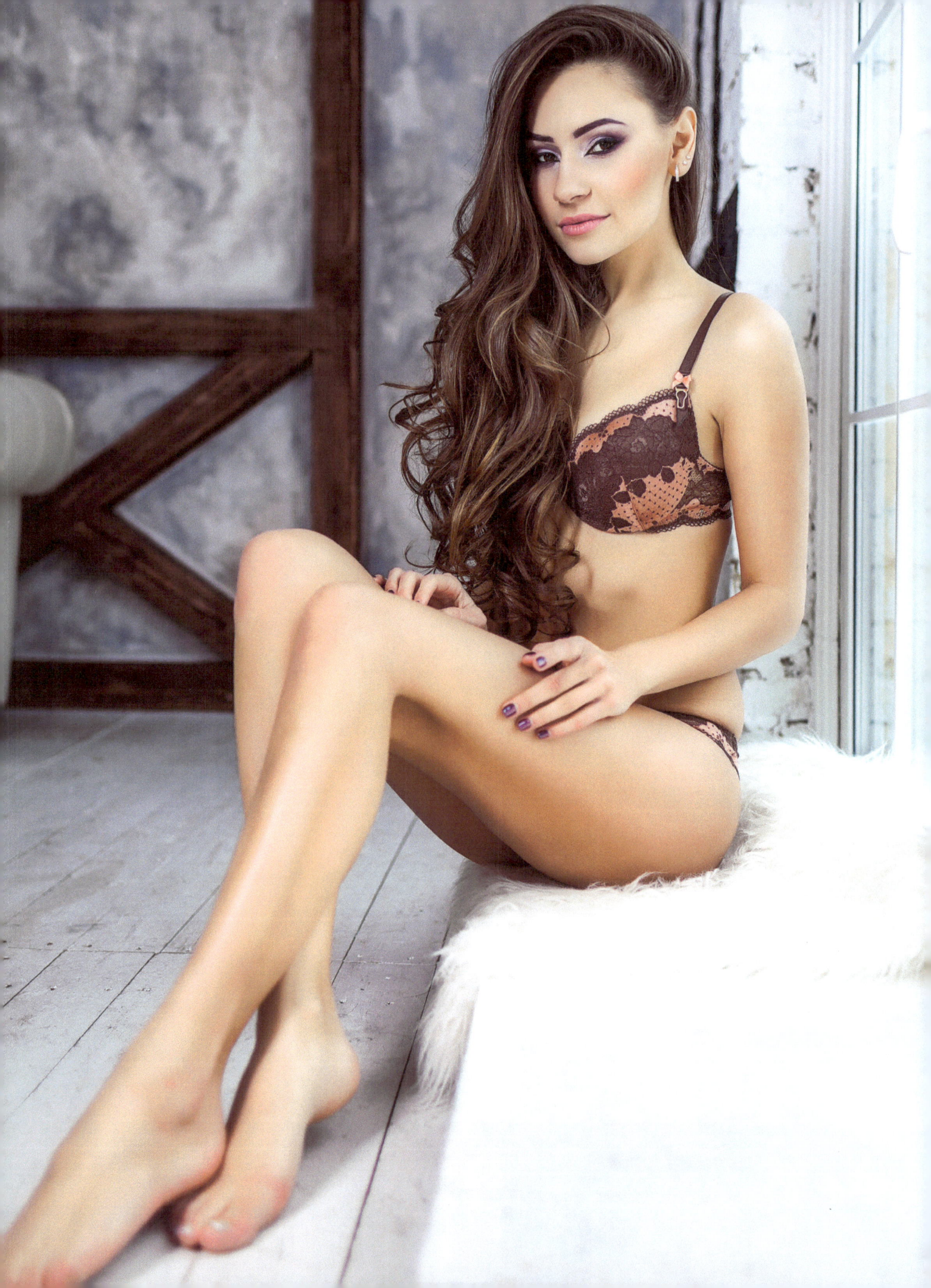

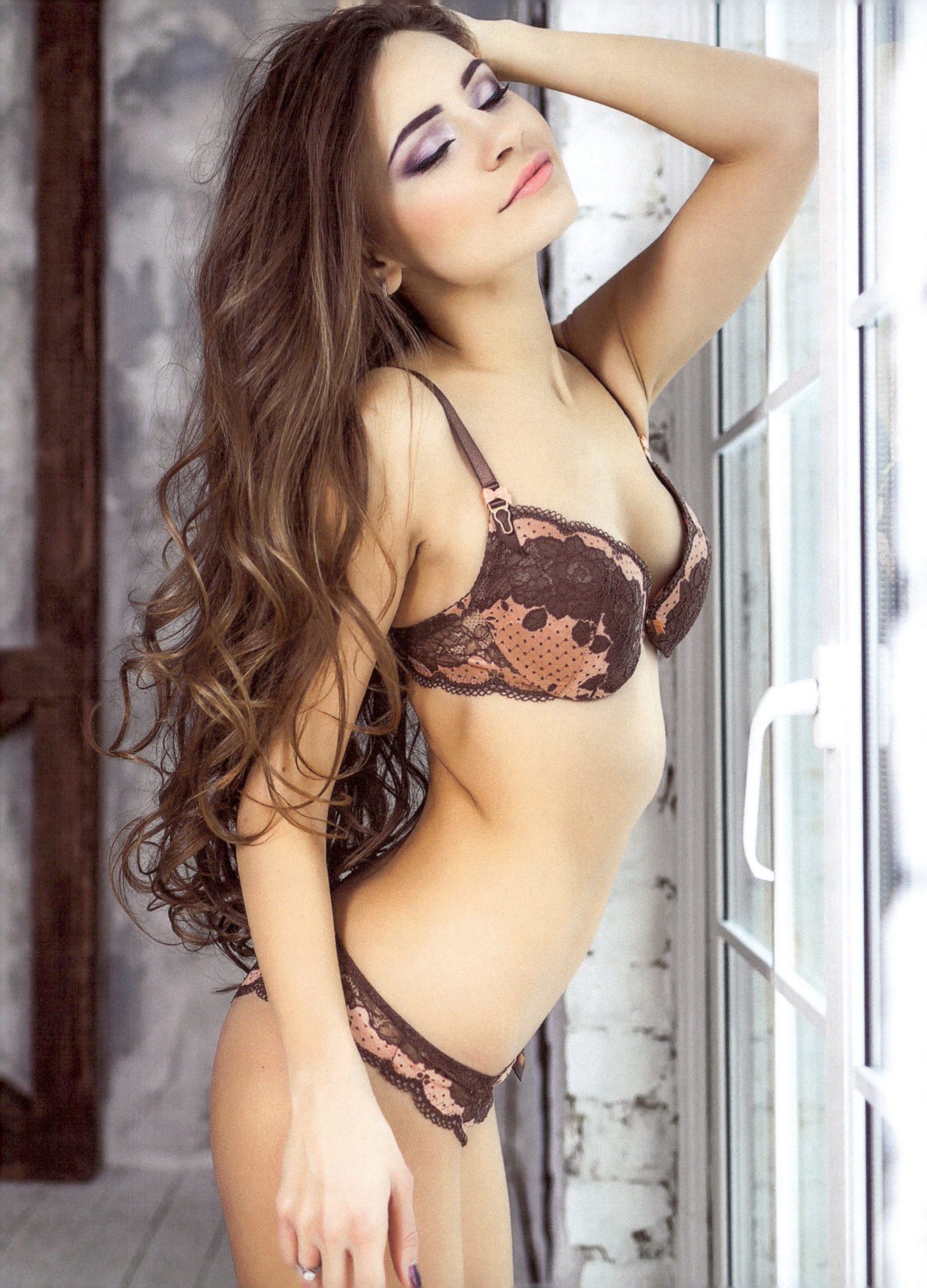

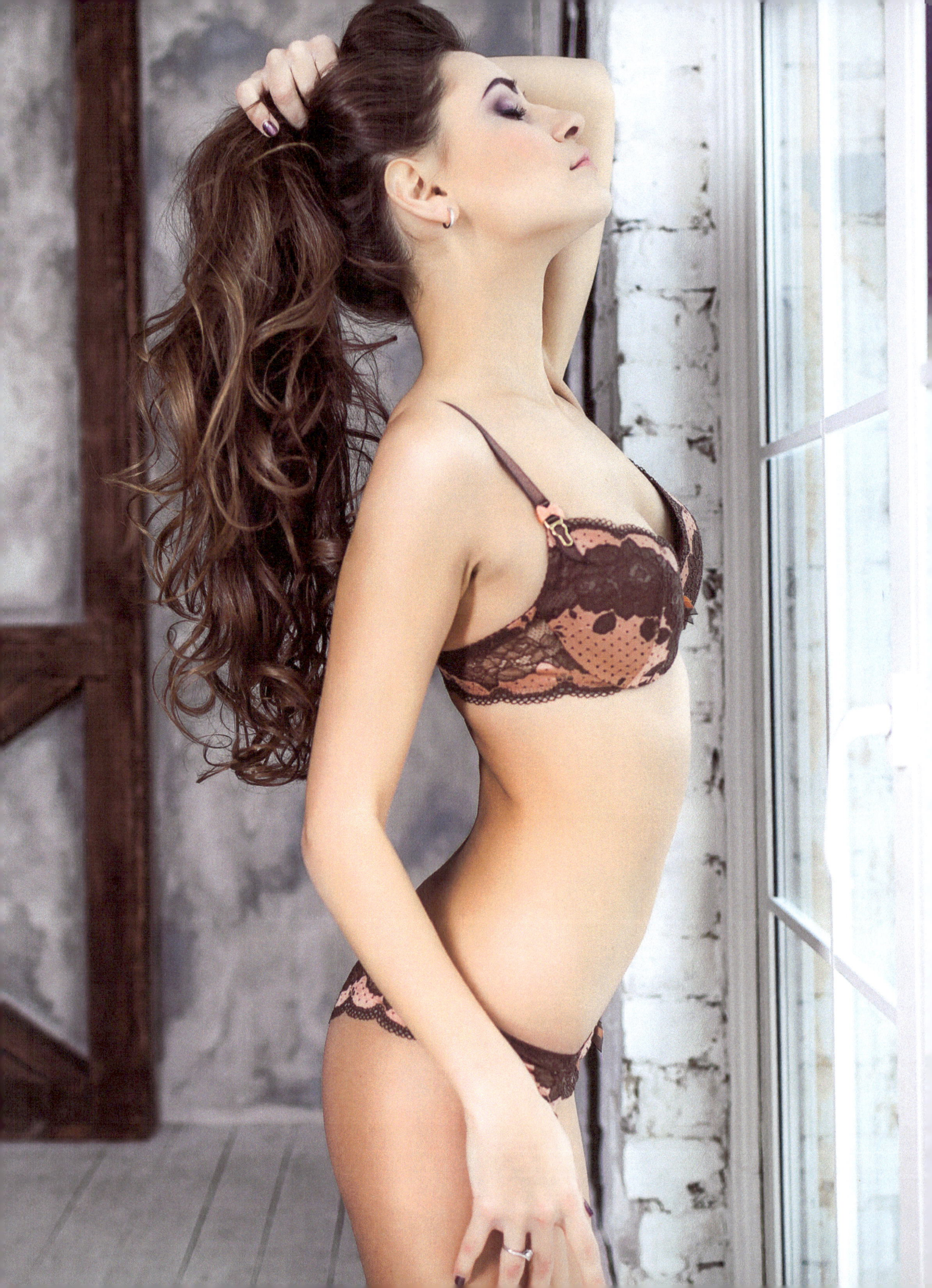

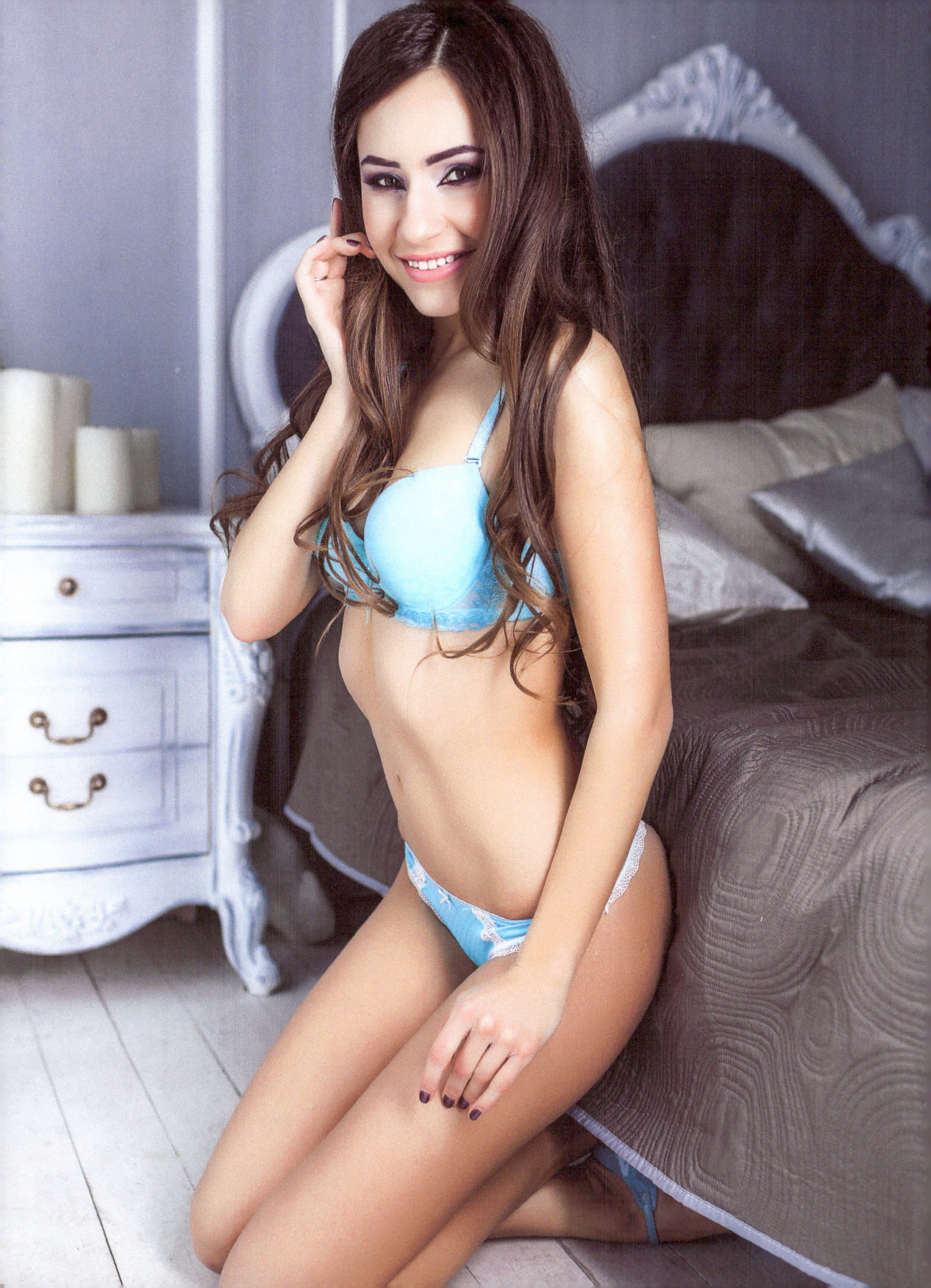

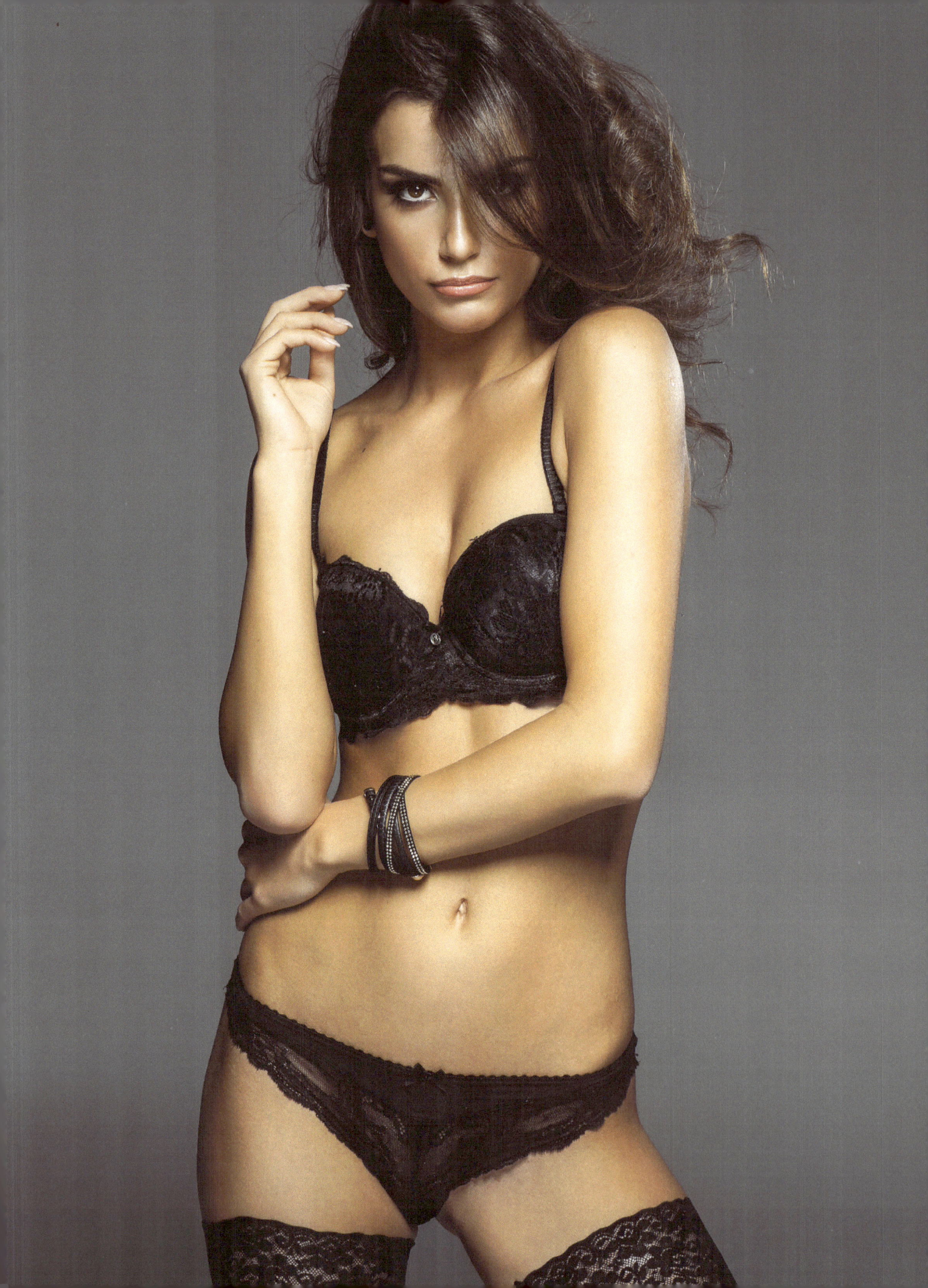

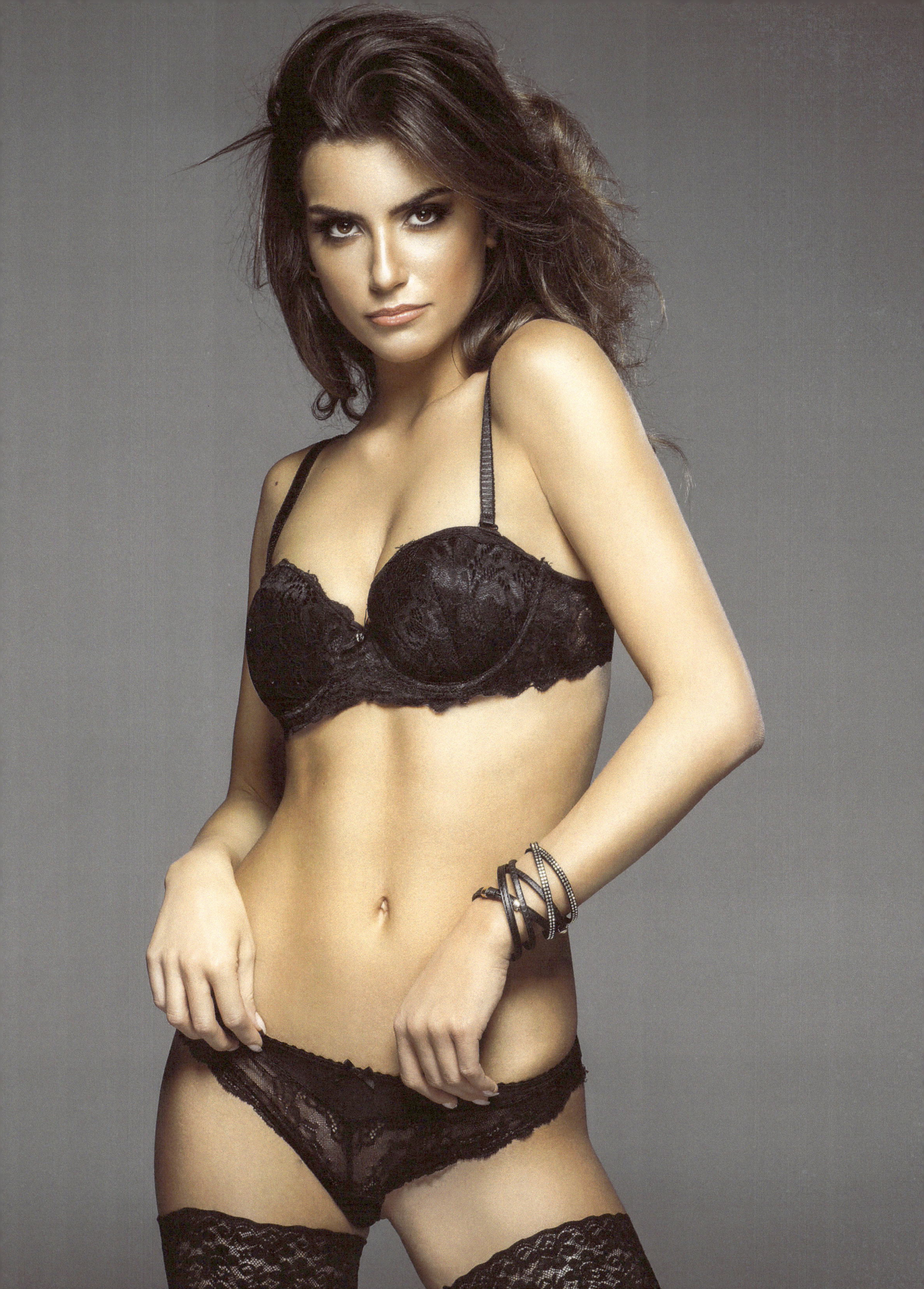

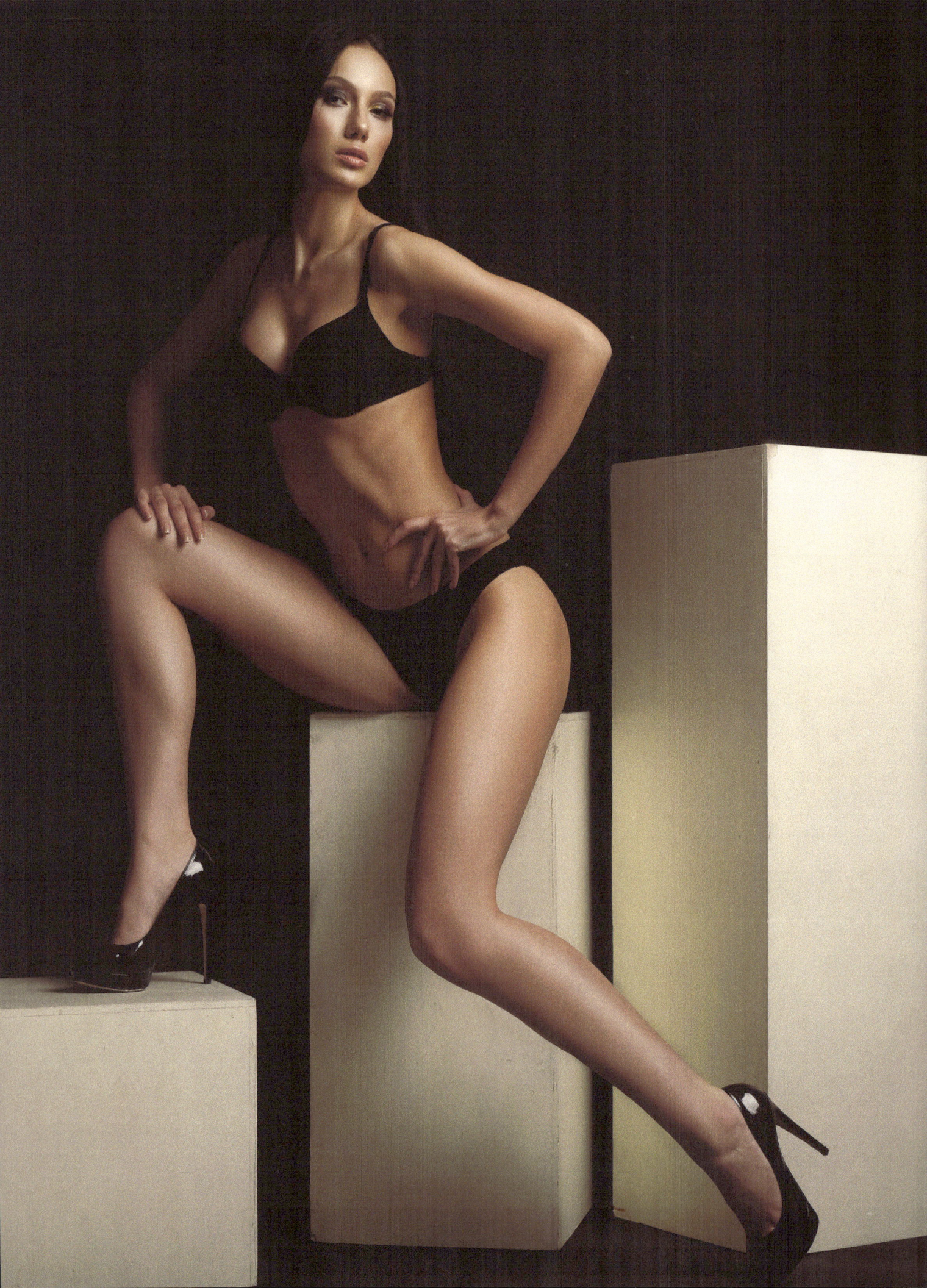

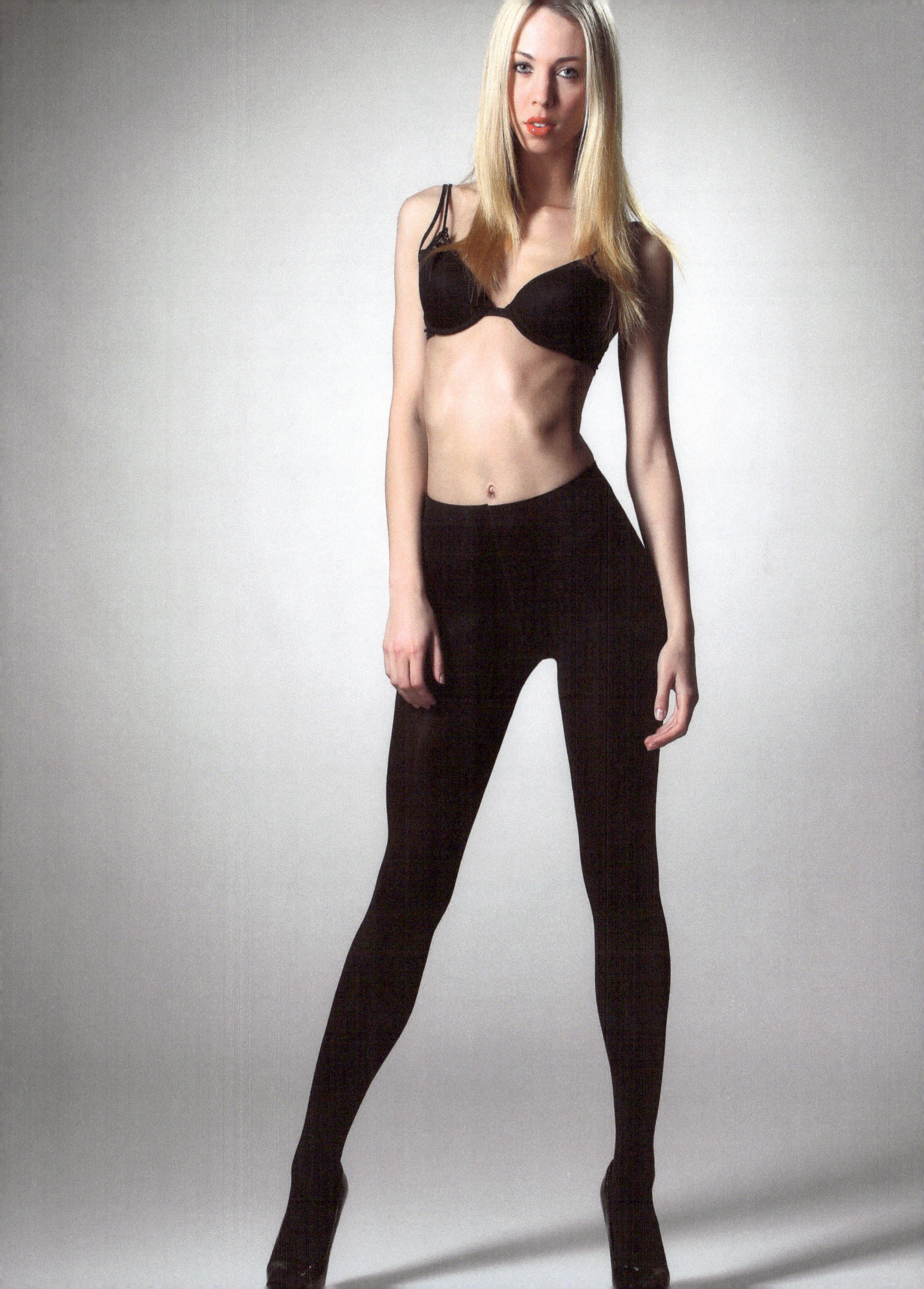

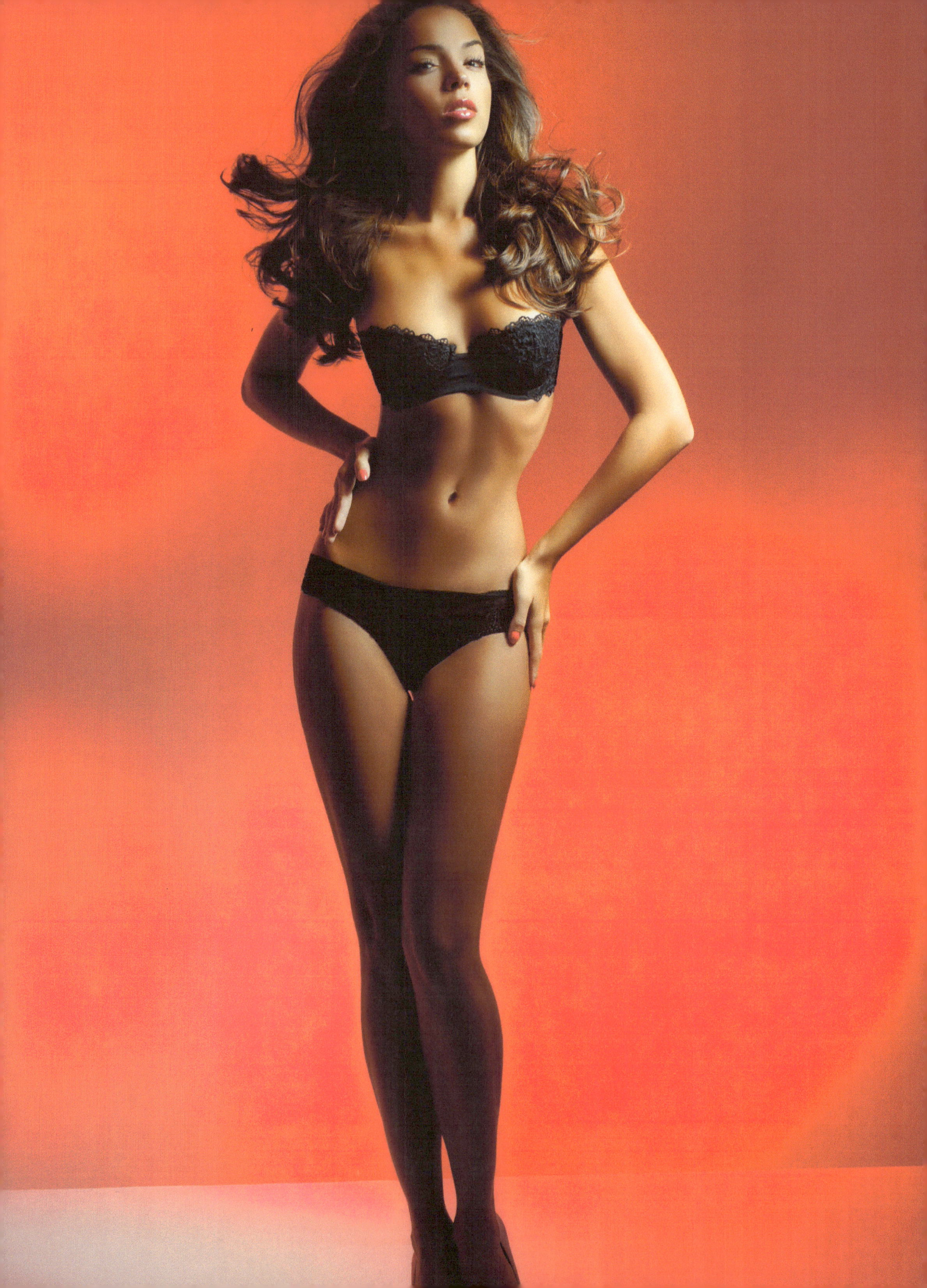

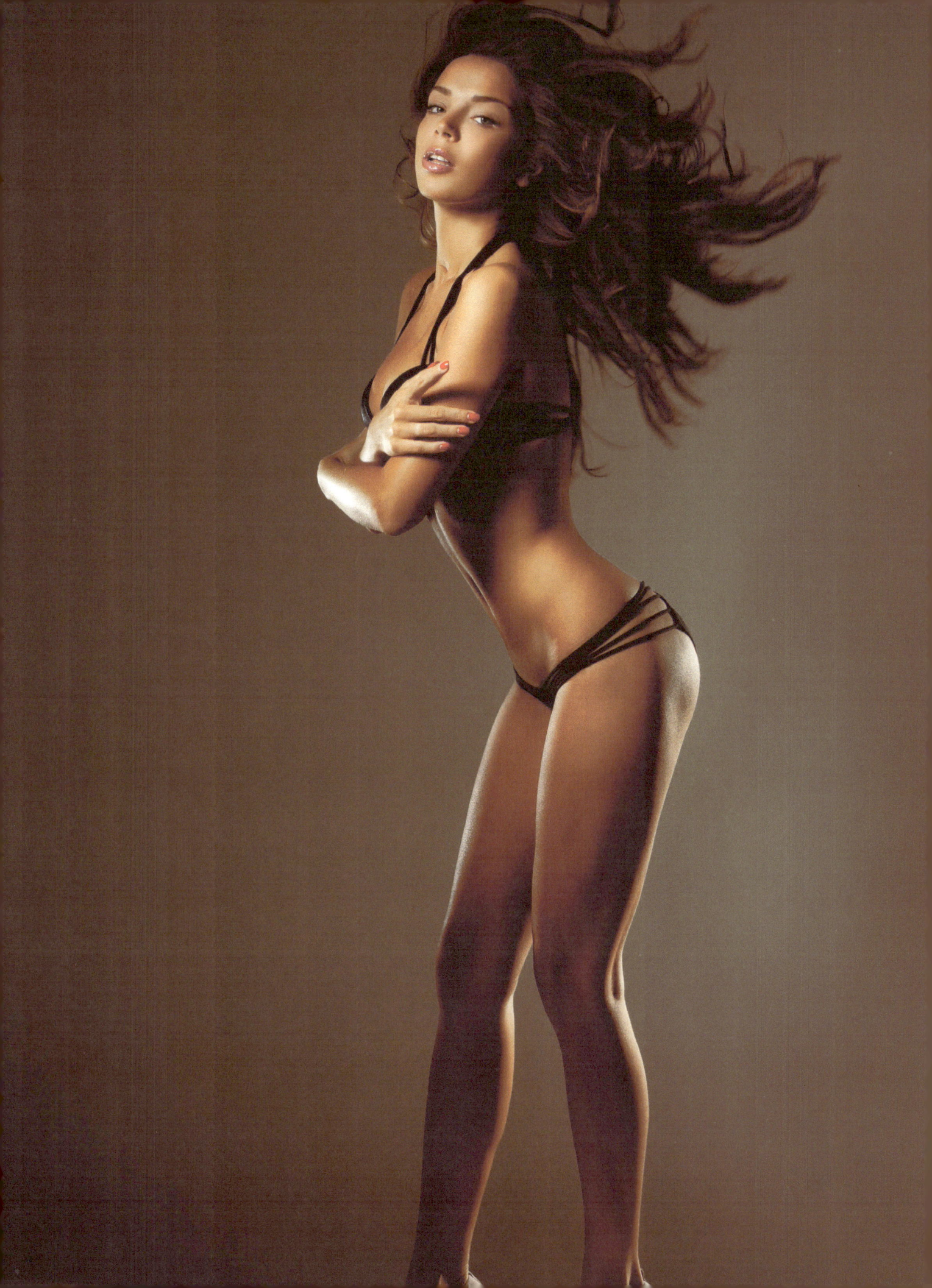

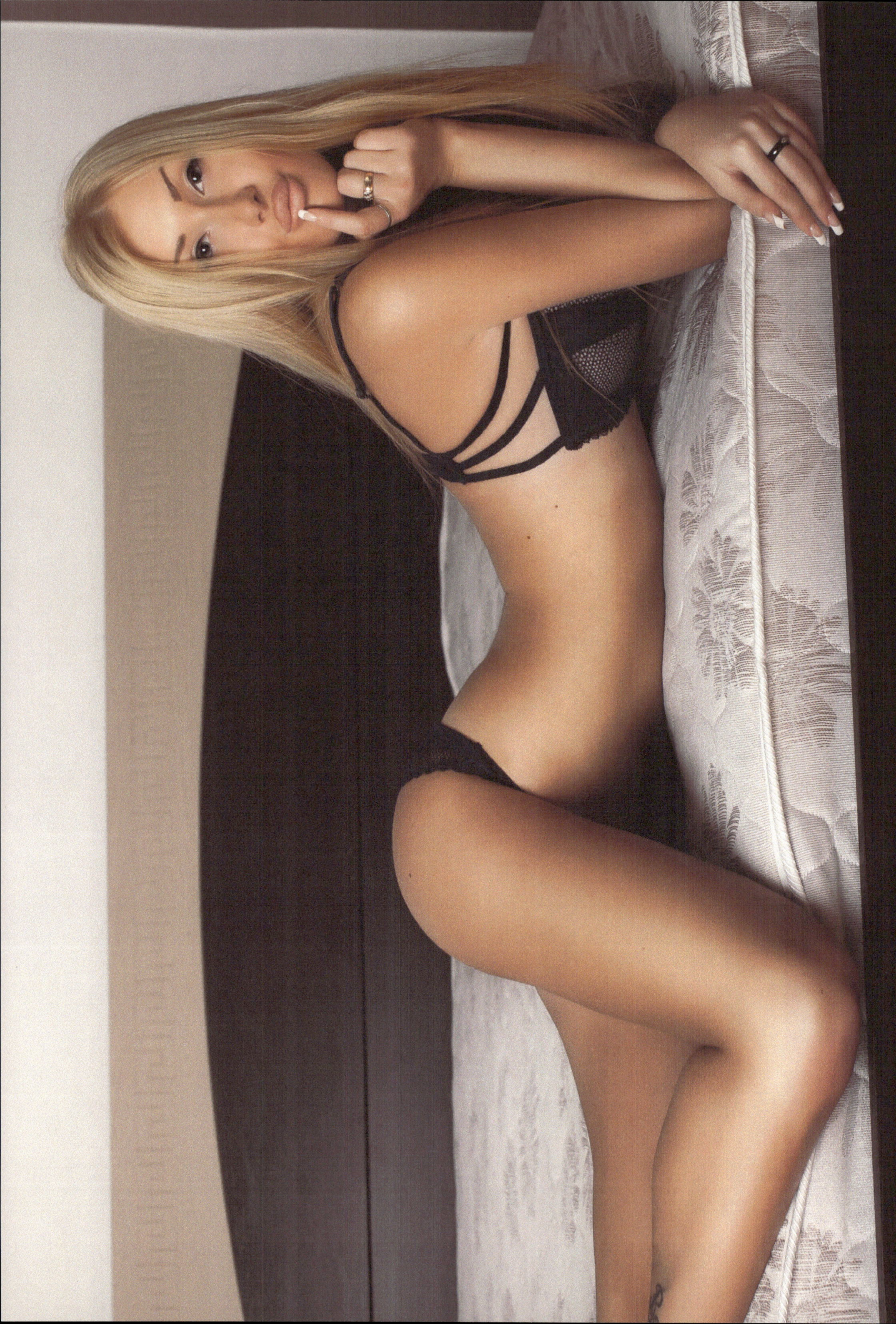

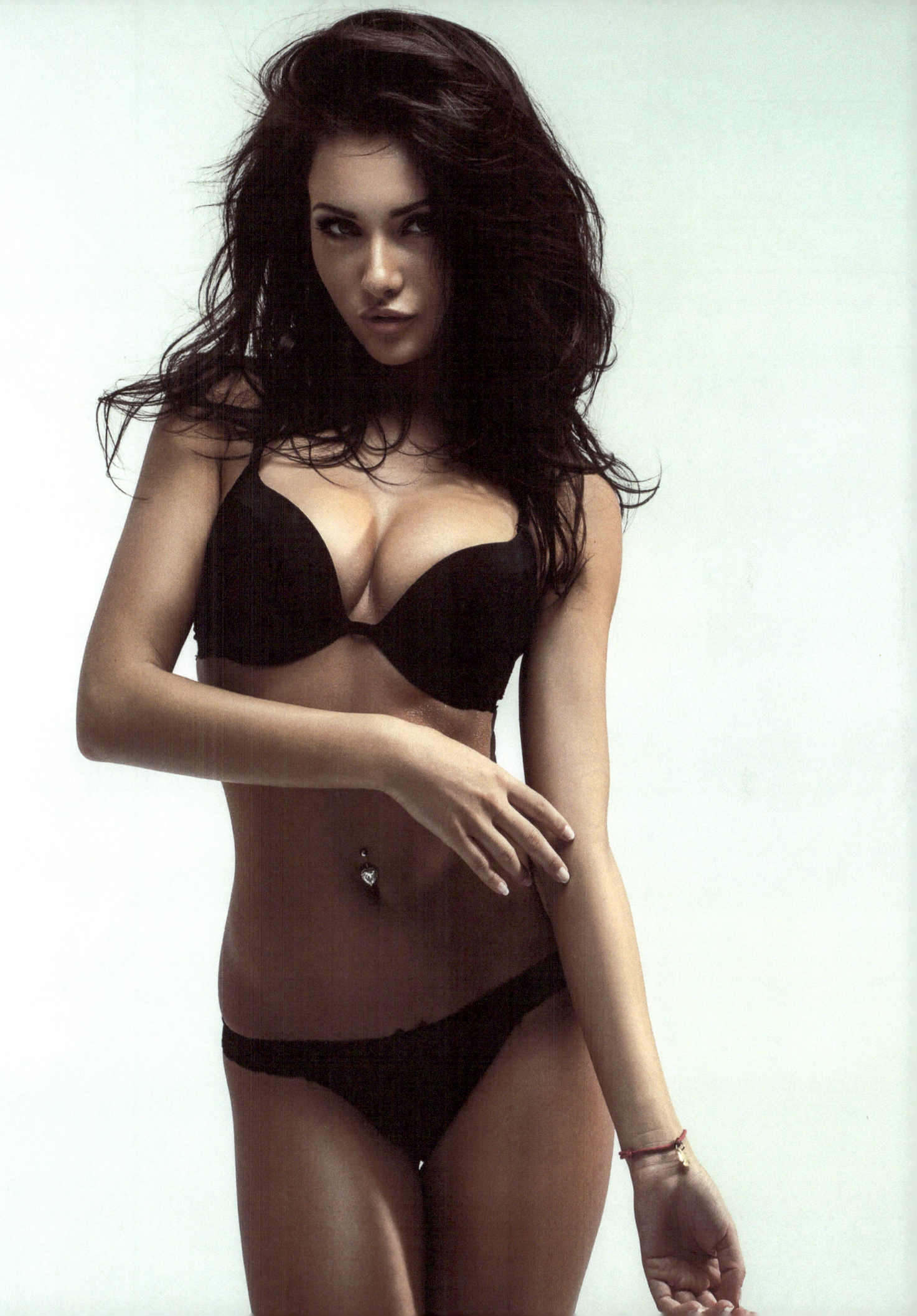

www.ingramcontent.com/pod-product-compliance
Lightning Source LLC
Chambersburg PA
CBHW050422180526
45159CB00005B/2371